Competitive Equity

Competitive Equity

A Better Way to Organize
Mutual Funds

Peter J. Wallison and Robert E. Litan

The AEI Press

Publisher for the American Enterprise Institute

WASHINGTON, D.C.

Distributed to the Trade by National Book Network, 15200 NBN Way, Blue Ridge Summit, PA 17214. To order call toll free 1-800-462-6420 or 1-717-794-3800. For all other inquiries please contact the AEI Press, 1150 Seventeenth Street, N.W., Washington, D.C. 20036 or call 1-800-862-5801.

Library of Congress Cataloging-in-Publication Data

Wallison, Peter J.
    Competitive Equity : a better way to organize mutual funds / Peter J. Wallison and Robert E. Litan.
        p. cm.
    Includes bibliographical references and index.
    ISBN-13: 978-0-8447-4252-6
    ISBN-10: 0-8447-4252-X
    1. Mutual funds—United States—Management. 2. Investment analysis—United States. I. Litan, Robert E., 1950– II. Title.

    HG4930.W355 2007
    9332.63'27—dc22

                                                                    2007008136

11 10 09 08 07   1 2 3 4 5

Printed in the United States of America

Contents

List of Illustrations

Acknowledgments

The authors wish to thank Daniel F. Geary of the American Enterprise Institute for his extraordinary and invaluable assistance in the work of researching, writing, and editing this book.

The authors also wish to thank the following people who participated as presenters or discussants in AEI conferences that assisted in the preparation of this book: Barry P. Barbash, T. Neil Bathon, Geoffrey H. Bobroff, John C. Bogle, Pierre Bollon, Todd J. Broms, Matthew A. Chambers, Warren Cormier, Rebecca A. Cowdery, Robert G. Dorsey, Susan C. Ervin, Melanie L. Fein, Matthew P. Fink, Gary L. Gastineau, Sander R. Gerber, Robert Hoffmann, John M. Kimpel, Martin E. Lybecker, Jerry W. Markham, Kathryn B. McGrath, James D. McLaughlin, David K. Musto, Donald J. Myers, Robert C. Pozen, John D. Rea, Daniel J. Roth, Paul F. Roye, David S. Ruder, Richard Saunders, Michael S. Scofield, Michael J. Sharp, Marianne K. Smythe, Paul S. Stevens, Paula A. Tkac, Steven M. H. Wallman, Stephen K. West, and David L. Wray.

The financial support of several investment advisory groups made ten public conferences at which the views of many interested groups were solicited and expressed. Nevertheless, no one connected with the mutual fund industry reviewed the text of this book prior to its publication, or collaborated in the development of its conclusions and recommendations. Accordingly, only the authors are responsible for any errors that it might contain.

1

A New Look at Mutual Funds

Over the last thirty years, with the elimination of rate regulation in several major industries, the American economy has undergone an immense change. As the government withdrew from the business of regulating the prices charged by airlines, interstate telecommunications firms, trucking companies, banks, and securities brokerages, among others, prices in these industries have fallen, new entrants have come on the scene, and innovation has flourished.

Yet in one industry, larger than any of these and arguably as important to the future well-being of American families, a form of rate regulation remains in force, suppressing price competition and keeping prices for many consumers above what a competitive market would produce. That industry is the mutual funds industry.

Mutual funds are companies that pool the savings of many investors and invest them in stocks, bonds, and other securities, thus allowing small investors to diversify and benefit from professional investment management at a reasonable cost. Most U.S. mutual funds today are organized as corporations, with boards of directors ultimately responsible for their operations. In almost all cases, however, funds have no staff or management of their own. Instead, each fund is managed by an investment adviser under a management contract approved by its board and shareholders.

The cost to an investor of owning shares of a mutual fund is the adviser's fee for managing the fund's portfolio, plus all the expenses that the adviser incurs in operating the fund under the management contract. These expenses include the fees of the transfer agent, the custodian, and the fund's auditors, as well as the cost of maintaining the books and records of the fund. The sum of these expenses, stated as a percentage of the fund's total assets, is called the fund's expense ratio. (Some funds also impose a sales charge, or load, when shares are purchased or redeemed; this is not included in the expense ratio.) The expense ratio can be thought of as the price that the adviser charges to operate the fund—and it is this price that is subject to regulation.

The idea that mutual fund prices are regulated will come as a surprise to many, since the Securities and Exchange Commission (SEC), which regulates mutual funds as well as the rest of the U.S. securities industry, has no explicit authority to regulate rates. But the rates of mutual funds are regulated not by the SEC but by the funds' boards of directors, which approve the investment advisers' fees and expenses each year. As discussed in detail in chapter 4, the way a mutual fund adviser's fees and expenses are presented to and approved by the fund's board does not differ substantially from the way rates are established by the public utility commissions that regulate the pricing of, say, electricity in local communities. Taking the adviser's fees and expenses as the "rate base," a fund's board allows what the directors believe to be a reasonable profit, and the sum of these fees, expenses, and allowed profit becomes the maximum that the adviser may charge the fund's shareholders.

This approach to price setting, as we will show, suppresses cost cutting, and thus price competition, among investment advisers just as effectively as it suppresses cost cutting by electric utilities. We will then propose an alternative approach that we believe will foster competition among investment advisers, spur innovation, and lower the costs of mutual funds for all investors. But first, it is worth explaining why price deregulation in the mutual fund industry is an important public policy issue.

Why Mutual Funds

One of the most basic rules of personal finance is never to put all of one's financial eggs in one basket. Financial experts unanimously encourage investors to lower their risks by purchasing stocks of different companies in different industries, and indeed to diversify across asset classes, to include bonds and real estate as well as equities, and even across countries. This advice follows from the efficient market hypothesis, which holds that no single investor can have more information at any given moment than is in the market as a whole, and therefore no investor, no matter how skilled, can consistently "beat the market" in picking individual securities.

Accordingly, in an era when most Americans must save for their retirement themselves, through defined-contribution pensions and other personal tax-advantaged savings plans, there is an urgent need for a collective investment vehicle that will enable them to diversify their holdings inexpensively. Mutual funds, by spreading the cost of investment advisory services over a large number of investors, have the potential to be the lowest-cost form of diversification.

In the early years of the last century, the only way an investor could diversify was to acquire a portfolio of stocks and bonds directly. Because brokerage fees for small stock purchases were relatively high, only those few individuals who had substantial financial means could hope to acquire enough different securities to achieve diversification at a reasonable cost. In the 1920s, however, two variations of a new collective investment vehicle developed in the United States. One, and initially the most popular, was the closed-end investment company, which was structured as a corporation and offered investors shares in a managed securities portfolio of a fixed size (hence the term "closed-end"). This new vehicle offered diversification, but with a significant drawback. Because an investor could divest his or her shares of the company only by selling them to another investor, the price received could differ from what the corresponding share of the company's portfolio was worth. Indeed, closed-end company shares usually traded at a discount from the per-share net asset value (NAV) of the portfolio.

The second new variant, the open-end investment company, or mutual fund, offered a more efficient structure. Also structured as a corporation (or in some cases a business trust), open-end funds issued new shares as investors demanded them and stood ready to redeem these shares at their NAV. This arrangement permitted shareholders to leave the fund at any time by seeking redemption of their shares at a price that was published daily in the newspaper.

Both types of investment company grew rapidly from their early beginnings. Until the Depression, roughly 95 percent of the $3 billion that the industry attracted was invested in closed-end funds. By 1929 there were many more closed-end funds (89) than open-end funds (19).[1] The stock market crash in October of that year changed all this, in large part because investors in closed-end funds had far more difficulty getting out of them than the investors who had bought mutual fund shares. Ever since then, mutual funds have grown increasingly popular, to the point where they are now an industry with over $10 trillion in assets under management, roughly 50 percent more than the deposits in all U.S. banks combined.

Several factors explain this extraordinary growth, including the increasing popularity of investment in equities, the rise in value of stocks generally, and the tax-advantaged savings programs approved by Congress, such as Individual Retirement Accounts and 401(k) plans, which encouraged diversified long-term investment for retirement. But innovative fund managers also encouraged the industry's growth by developing new ways of investing and diversifying that proved attractive to investors. One example was the index fund, whose portfolio tracks a broad stock market index such as the Standard & Poor's 500 or the Wilshire 5000. These funds are less expensive than actively managed funds because they do not require active investment research and stock selection. Management of an index fund consists only of matching the composition of the fund's portfolio with that of the index it mimics.[2]

The growth of index funds calls attention to the question of cost. Diversification, as noted, is not the only purpose for owning a mutual fund. There are, after all, other ways to create a diversified portfolio of stocks—separately managed accounts created by brokerage firms are an example—but all of them are likely to be less accessible than mutual funds to ordinary investors because they require more customized and hence more expensive management. What is unique about mutual funds is their second main advantage: their ability to allow small investors to participate in the potentially high returns of investment in securities at low cost. It follows that a primary goal of public policy should be to ensure that nothing unnecessarily hinders fund managers from offering the lowest possible costs to investors. We believe this can best be done by creating an environment in which mutual funds and other collective investment vehicles can operate as efficiently as possible.

An important reason for this focus on mutual fund costs is that the long-term consequences of even small differences in cost can be considerable. Figure 1-1 shows that there are significant differences in expense ratios among mutual funds. Although the ratios themselves seem small—ranging roughly from 60 basis points (0.6 percent of fund assets) to 170 basis points (1.7 percent) per year—the differences among them add up over time. John Bogle, founder of the Vanguard Group of mutual funds and one of the industry's severest critics, notes in a recent book that, in the ten-year period between March 1, 1995, and February 28, 2005, a $1 investment in the average mutual fund in the lowest-cost fund quartile would have grown by $2.07, but by only $1.18 in the average fund in the highest-cost quartile.[3] Over a lifetime of investment, such differences can have a substantial effect on the size of an investor's retirement nest egg. Although, as we explain later, we do not agree with Bogle's diagnosis of the industry's problems or with his prescription for reform, we do not disagree with the numbers he presents—or at least their general direction. Relatively small differences in cost can indeed produce large differences in outcome over the course of an investment lifetime.

Rate Regulation by Mutual Fund Boards of Directors Impairs Competition and Keeps Mutual Fund Prices High

Although many other formerly rate-regulated industries now set their prices through competition, the mutual fund industry has seen no significant deregulation since the adoption of its governing law, the Investment Company Act of 1940 (ICA). In fact, mutual funds are, if anything, more heavily regulated today than when the ICA was enacted. As described in chapter 2, the ICA assumes that mutual funds will be established and maintained in corporate form, and it requires the boards of directors of these corporations to approve the costs that investors must pay for the collective investment services of the fund adviser.

This regime has a major effect on pricing and competition. For example, under the ICA and the SEC's regulations, boards of directors are expected to request that advisers reduce their advisory fees as the fund grows in size. This process, which is called adding fee "breakpoints," is intended to take account of the increasing economies of scale that the adviser supposedly achieves from managing a larger fund. However, as discussed below, the expectation that boards will seek to lower fees as the fund grows dramatically changes the adviser's pricing incentives.

As noted, investment advisers to mutual funds are compensated through a fee that is set as a percentage of the fund's assets. Thus an adviser seeking to increase its total compensation might consider doing so by lowering the fund's expense ratio so as to attract more investors and so increase the fund's assets. However, under the existing rate regulation system, pursuing this strategy entails a major risk for which the adviser may not be compensated. If the lower expense ratio fails to attract more investors, the adviser's revenue and profit will fall, but if it succeeds, the board of directors will seek to add breakpoints to the adviser's fee. Thus the adviser may be deprived of at least some of the profit resulting from this risk taking. This system surely has an adverse effect on price competition among investment advisory firms and their desire to increase market share through cutting fees and expenses.

One way to think about this is to imagine that an excess profits tax has been imposed on all airline profits over a certain level. If an airline wants to raise its revenue and profit on a particular route, it may lower its prices in the belief that this will attract enough new passengers to more than make up for the lower prices. This involves some risk, because the lower prices may instead result in reduced revenue and profits if other airlines also lower their rates or if passengers simply fail to respond by switching from higher-priced competitors. But the excess profits tax requires the airline to take another risk. Even if it is successful in attracting more passengers, some or all of the added profits will be taxed away. In other words, the airline will not be fully compensated for the risk of lowering its prices; some of the gains will be siphoned off by the tax. Any airline in this situation will think twice before lowering its prices and might decide that the risk is not worth the cost. In the same way, investment advisers are discouraged by break-points from lowering their costs.

Other, perhaps more important obstacles to price cutting arise from the fact that investment advisers must annually justify their fees and expenses to a board of directors. In the time-honored way for rate-regulated industries, investment advisers report their costs to the directors, who, in the same time-honored way, then allow what they regard as a reasonable profit—ordinarily as a percentage of the costs. But what costs do advisers report? Obviously, they report their *actual* costs—all their costs of serving all their customers—or what economists would call their fully allocated average costs.

But this is not the relevant cost of a company in a competitive market. In a competitive market, the relevant cost of a competitor is *marginal cost*—what it will cost to serve *the last customer who can be served at a profit*. And in most competitive markets this cost is much lower than the average cost of serving all customers. This fact (which is literally textbook microeconomics)[4] is critical to understanding pricing in the mutual fund industry. Since, as noted, boards of directors generally add a reasonable profit allowance onto the costs they are shown by the fund's adviser, there is no incentive for the adviser to provide to the board anything but its average cost, which of course results in a higher allowable profit than the adviser's marginal cost would produce.

This is not to say that investment advisers are hiding their marginal cost from their boards of directors. In fact, fund advisers *cannot* report their marginal cost to their boards, because *they do not know what their marginal costs actually are*. Only a business actually engaged in competition can know its marginal cost because only then is it required to seek out the least expensive way to serve that last profitable customer. That is why Friedrich Hayek, in a famous essay, called competition "a discovery procedure":[5] it is competition, and competition alone, that pushes a company to discover how to deliver its products most efficiently. In the mutual fund world, where virtually all advisers must receive approval of their fees and expenses from a board of directors, there is, as noted, no incentive for them to discover all the innovations or efficiencies that would reduce their costs. If they did, the board, adding a "reasonable" profit to the lower cost figures presented to them, would simply reduce the adviser's fee accordingly.

It is in this sense that the regulation of mutual fund pricing bears a strong resemblance to the way rates are established by electric and other utilities. In both cases the price of the service is determined by the regulatory body allowing what it regards as a reasonable profit in relation to the costs reported by the regulated company. And this explains why, in the mutual fund industry as in electric utility pricing, one does not see the wholesale cost and price cutting observed in other industries that have been relieved of government regulation and forced to compete on price. Some may argue that the analogy to electric utility regulation is inapposite because electric utilities are natural monopolies and face no competition, whereas mutual funds and their advisers function in a market that has at least a competitive structure, consisting of dozens if not hundreds of mutual fund groups or "families" and literally thousands of individual funds. But this objection misses the point: unless investment advisers are free to set their own prices for their services, they are not able to compete effectively on price, no matter how many "competitors" they have. This leads to some absurd situations. A headline in the *Wall Street Journal* not long ago declared, "Independent Directors Strike Back."[6] The article celebrated the fact that the independent directors of the funds operated by AIM Management were demanding that the funds lower their advisory fees. No one seemed to notice how odd it was that a board of directors would have to demand that a company's management lower its prices, but that was exactly what was happening. In an industry where competitors are free to set their prices, this would never happen; competition would drive prices down. In a competitive industry, boards are more likely to worry that prices are too low. But where prices are set in the same way as for electric utilities, the regulated firms behave like regulated utilities.

In overall structure, indeed, the mutual fund industry has all the attributes of a highly competitive market: ease of entry, a multitude of competing organizations, and a vast number of customers who are largely free to move from fund to fund in search of the best results. A recent study by two noted academics, John Coates and Glenn Hubbard, focuses heavily on the competitive structure of the industry to argue that it is in fact competitive,[7] and anyone who reads the financial pages of daily newspapers will see aggressive advertising by competing fund groups.

Yet, as shown below, there is strong evidence that the mutual fund industry is not as price-competitive as its structure would suggest. The expense ratios of funds that ostensibly compete with one another in fact vary widely.[8] The industry thus does not appear to conform to the "law of one price"[9]—that is, the prices of the collective investment services that mutual funds provide are not converging toward a common level, although convergence would be expected in a competitive market.

Figure 1-1 illustrates this price dispersion for one large sector of the U.S. mutual fund industry, the class A shares of 811 actively managed equity funds. Class A shares generally have an initial (front-end), one-time sales charge or "load" of about 5 percent and charge a small annual 12b-1 fee to the fund itself (to cover distribution and related expenses) of about 0.25 percent (25 basis points). (As noted above, the front-end load is not included in the expense ratio, but the 12b-1 fee is.) To present a clearer picture of the dispersion of expenses for the manager's services alone, exclusive of distribution costs, we subtracted 25 basis points from each fund's expense ratio. In addition, to exclude outliers, we eliminated 3 percent of the funds at each end of the distribution. With these adjustments, the expense ratios of the 811 funds range from approximately 60 basis points to 170 basis points, or a difference in cost of almost 300 percent.

FIGURE 1-1

DISTRIBUTION OF EXPENSE RATIOS OF CLASS A SHARES OF U.S. EQUITY MUTUAL FUNDS (811 Funds)

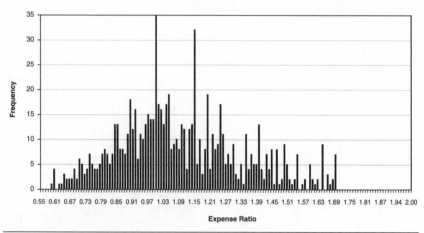

SOURCE: Morningstar, http://www.morningstar.com (accessed December 7, 2006).
NOTE: Data are for 811 funds as of December 7, 2006. All expense ratios are net 25 bps to account for 12b-1 (distribution) charges.

Of course, it is always possible that differences in the services these funds offer account for this wide dispersion in pricing, but we believe this is unlikely. Most competitive industries do have differences in service or product quality that account for some dispersion in pricing, but we doubt that any other industry with such a similar product exhibits the disparities shown in figure 1-1. Nor is it likely that some unique feature of the collective investment industry accounts for this dispersion. For comparison, figure 1-2 shows the dispersion of expense ratios for 456 U.K. funds invested in U.K. or U.S. equities (again with the highest and the lowest 3 percent eliminated). The dispersion in the U.K. funds is much narrower than that in the U.S. funds, ranging from 127 to 196 basis points, a price difference of only 54 percent. We were unable to determine whether the U.K. funds also have an imbedded 25-basis-point 12b-1 fee. If, on the assumption that they do, and one subtracts 25 basis points as we did with the U.S. funds, the dispersion in the U.K. funds widens somewhat, but only to 68 percent—still substantially smaller than the U.S. dispersion.

FIGURE 1-2
**DISTRIBUTION OF EXPENSE RATIOS OF U.K. EQUITY
MUTUAL FUNDS (456 Funds)**

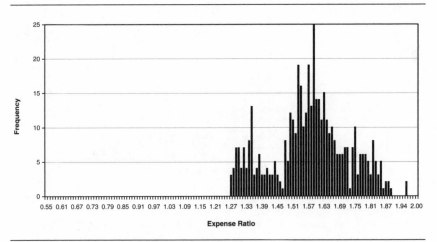

SOURCE: Investment Management Association, December 2005.
NOTE: Data are for 456 funds as of December 2005.

In the United Kingdom, mutual funds are generally contractual arrangements directly between advisers and investors; intervening corporate structures, where they exist, have no voice in the setting of the fees and expenses of advisers, which are able to set their own rates. As a result, investment advisers in the United Kingdom have incentives to compete and to find the lowest marginal cost that will attract the last profitable investor. In chapters 4 and 5 we borrow from this feature of the U.K. mutual fund landscape in fashioning our own recommendations for establishing an alternative collective investment model for the United States.

It might be objected that figure 1-2 also shows that U.K. funds are, on the whole, about 50 basis points more costly than U.S. funds. However, we do not regard this as particularly significant for purposes of our analysis, for three reasons. First, U.K. funds are considerably smaller on average than U.S. funds. According to a recent analysis by the mutual fund research group Lipper, the average U.K. fund is about one-fifth the size of the average U.S. fund ($688 million versus $3.2 billion).[10] This in itself would account for substantial differences in overall cost. Second, there is nothing about the structure of the collective investment industry in Britain that would suggest that it is inherently a more costly way to carry on that business. Third, because the U.S. equity market is much larger than the U.K. market, the U.K. funds are likely to be more invested in non-U.K. equities than U.S. funds are invested in non-U.S. equities, and this may add to the costs of U.K. advisers: U.S. funds that invest exclusively or mostly in non-U.S. companies tend to have higher expenses than those that do not. In any case, the point of our interest in the U.K. market structure is that the narrow dispersion in the pricing of U.K. funds clearly indicates price competition, suggesting that costs would be driven down substantially if the same environment prevailed in the United States.

It is worth noting that the disparity in pricing we find among U.S. funds extends even to the largest and presumably the most competitive fund families. If U.S. funds were truly price-competitive, it would be here that one would see the convergence toward one price that is characteristic of markets in which price competition prevails. Yet we do not see convergence even among this group. Table 1-1 presents expense ratios for several funds offered by the ten largest mutual fund families in the United States, showing that the dispersion in costs even among these funds ranges from over 100 percent to somewhat more than 200 percent.

The SEC's Failed Diagnosis

The unusual price dispersion among U.S. mutual funds has been noticed for a long time and has been attributed either to the failure of the funds' independent directors to control the expenses charged by investment advisers, or

TABLE 1-1

EXPENSE RATIOS OF REPRESENTATIVE LARGE-CAP FUNDS
OF THE TEN LARGEST U.S. FUND FAMILIES

Value Fund		
Fund Family	**Fund and Ticker Symbol**	**Expense Ratio**
Fidelity Investments	Fidelity Equity-Income II (FEQTX)	0.62
Vanguard Group	Vanguard Equity-Income (VEIPX)	0.31
Capital Research & Management	American Funds Investment Company of America A (AIVSX)	0.55
Franklin Templeton Investments	Franklin Equity Income A (FISEX)	0.93
Columbia Management Group	Columbia Large Cap Value A (NVLEX)	0.96
J.P. Morgan Chase & Co.	JPMorgan Value Opportunities A (JVOAX)	1.07
Morgan Stanley	Morgan Stanley Value A (VLUAX)	0.97
OppenheimerFunds/ MassMutual	Oppenheimer Value A (CGRWX)	0.99
TIAA-CREF	No representative fund	—
Federated Investors	Federated Equity-Income A (LEIFX)	1.11

Blend Fund		
Fund Family	**Fund and Ticker Symbol**	**Expense Ratio**
Fidelity Investments	Fidelity Fund (FFIDX)	0.56
Vanguard Group	Vanguard Growth & Income (VQNPX)	0.37
Capital Research & Management	No representative fund	—
Franklin Templeton Investments	Franklin Growth A (FKGRX)	0.94
Columbia Management Group	Columbia Large Cap Enhanced Core A (NMIAX)	0.75
J.P. Morgan Chase & Co.	JPMorgan Disciplined Equity A (JDEAX)	0.85
Morgan Stanley	Morgan Stanley Dividend Growth Securities B (DIVBX)	0.75
OppenheimerFunds/ MassMutual	Oppenheimer Main Street A (MSIGX)	0.92
TIAA-CREF	TIAA-CREF Growth & Income (TIGIX)	0.43
Federated Investors	Federated Capital Appreciation A (FEDEX)	1.22

continued on next page

Table 1-1 continued

Growth Fund		
Fund Family	Fund and Ticker Symbol	Expense Ratio
Fidelity Investments	Fidelity Blue Chip Growth (FBGRX)	0.64
Vanguard Group	Vanguard Morgan Growth (VMRGX)	0.39
Capital Research & Management	American Funds AMCAP A (AMCPX)	0.65
Franklin Templeton Investments	Franklin Capital Growth A (FKREX)	0.95
Columbia Management Group	Columbia Large Cap Growth A (LEGAX)	1.11
J.P. Morgan Chase & Co.	JPMorgan Large Cap Growth A (OLGAX)	1.24
Morgan Stanley	Morgan Stanley Focus Growth A (AMOAX)	1.01
OppenheimerFunds/ MassMutual	Oppenheimer Equity A (OEQAX)	0.89
TIAA-CREF	TIAA-CREF Growth Equity (TIGEX)	0.45
Federated Investors	Federated Large Cap Growth A (FLGAX)	1.45

SOURCE: Data from Morningstar, www.morningstar.com (accessed October 17, 2006).
NOTE: Data are as of October 17, 2006.

to inadequate disclosure of costs, or to both. In a June 2000 study of the mutual fund industry, for example, the Government Accountability Office (GAO) described the structure of the industry as one of "monopolistic competition,"[11] attributing the wide fee dispersion to inadequate disclosure.

But why should an industry with hundreds of competing advisers offering similar services (and little to prevent more from entering), thousands of funds, and millions of normally price-conscious customers exhibit limited or monopolistic competition? As noted above and detailed in later chapters, we believe the answer lies in the industry's legal and regulatory structure, which requires boards of directors to approve the fees and expenses of investment advisers. But for at least forty years the SEC's diagnosis of this problem has been different—and, we believe, flawed. Promoted by the agency with regulatory responsibility for the mutual fund industry, this flawed diagnosis has called forth a prescription that has simply made the symptoms worse.

Most of the current legal structure of mutual funds stems from an attempt by federal policymakers to curb what critics charged were a range of abuses by managers of closed-end funds in the 1920s and 1930s. In 1935 Congress directed the newly formed SEC to examine these charges, to study the entire "investment trust and investment company" industry, and to report recommendations for legislative action. The Commission responded in 1939 with an extensive analysis,[12] which ultimately led to the ICA. The act did not attempt to establish a more flexible or open-source structure for collective investment, but only to address the problems associated with the industry as it was then organized. The ICA simply assumed that mutual funds would be corporations or trusts, governed by boards of directors and usually managed by investment advisers under contractual arrangements.

By failing to make clear how it thought funds should be governed, Congress set up a structure in which conflicts about the control of mutual funds became inevitable. Under ordinary corporate law, the board of directors has ultimate responsibility for managing a company's affairs. Contractors, such as an investment adviser, have a subordinate role and are ultimately subject to control or dismissal by the board. However, because of the economics of the mutual fund industry, as will be outlined in chapter 2, only securities firms and investment advisers have incentives to pay the costs associated with setting up a mutual fund. Having done so, it is hardly unreasonable for an adviser to believe that it should have control of the fund it has created. Moreover, the business of a mutual fund is investing, and a board of directors is generally not as competent as the investment adviser to make the investment and trading decisions that are the fund's sole business.

In adopting the ICA, Congress never resolved the question of whether the investment adviser or the board of directors was to control the fund. It did not help matters that the ICA permitted the adviser to name a majority of the fund's board of directors, but placed important authority—especially approval of the investment advisory agreement—in the hands of the 40 percent of the board who were required to be independent of the adviser. The lack of clear focus on this issue by Congress was encapsulated in the differences between the Senate and House bills. The Senate draft required a majority of independent directors; the House bill contained a 40 percent requirement, and the House report warned that "a board with an independent majority would repudiate the recommendations of the adviser, depriving investment company shareholders of the benefits of those rec-ommendations."[13] The conference report adopted the House language, which became law.

The ambiguity was eliminated over time by the SEC, which ultimately came to the view that Congress had adopted a corporate structure deliber-ately for the purpose of protecting fund shareholders. "The role of directors in policing conflicts of interest is central to the Act," the SEC staff wrote in 1992, and "The independent directors, in particular, are expected to look after the interests of shareholders. . . ."[14] To the SEC this meant that the board has a responsibility to control and reduce the fees and the other expenses that the adviser charges to the fund. In the same report the SEC succinctly stated the issue as the agency had come to see it: "Fees paid from an investment company's assets to sponsors [usually the investment adviser] and their affiliates—whether advisers' fees, principal underwriting fees, distribution fees, or fees for other services—directly affect sharehold-ers' investment return. The higher the fee, the lower the return. The con-flict of interest is inherent."[15]

Thus the relatively high expense ratios charged by many funds were seen as a failure of the board to exercise sufficient control over the adviser, primarily because the board lacked sufficient bargaining power in negotiat-ing with the adviser over the adviser's fees and expenses. As one Senate report put it in 1969, "Since a typical fund is organized by its investment adviser which provides it with almost all management services and because its shares are bought by investors who rely on that service, a mutual fund cannot, as a practical matter sever its relationship with the adviser. *Therefore, the forces of arm's-length bargaining do not work in the mutual fund industry in the same manner as they do in other sectors of the American economy*" (emphasis added).[16] With this as its diagnosis for high fees and expenses, the SEC embarked on a campaign—still ongoing today—to strengthen the ability of the independent directors to confront and bargain with the adviser.

In 1970, at the urging of the SEC, Congress amended the ICA to add a provision formally imposing a "fiduciary duty" on the adviser, as well as the board, to act on the shareholders' behalf. This provision, section 36(b)—clearly the logical result of the idea that there is an inherent conflict of inter-est between adviser and fund—was designed to ensure that advisers' fees would be reasonable and not inconsistent with the interests of fund share-holders. As we will outline in greater detail in chapter 4, section 36(b) has produced the opposite result.

As figures 1-1 and 1-2 demonstrate, the SEC's regulatory approach has not been very successful. Despite the fact that boards have become much more independent of investment advisers, the dispersion of expense ratios is still very wide—much wider than in the United Kingdom, which does not have the same regulatory structure or rely on independent boards of directors to control the adviser's alleged conflicts of interest. If there is an "inherent conflict of interest" in the structure of mutual funds, giving greater authority and independence to boards of directors has not been able to address it. As two academic commentators noted, "This strangeness—tremendous popularity, proliferating consumer options, and less than robust price competition—arises in the realm of the most tightly regulated financial product sold in the country today. In the words of a former SEC chairman, 'no issuer of securities is subject to more detailed regulation than a mutual fund.'"[17] These commentators, like so many others, saw the coexistence of heavy regulation and lack of price competition as a paradox—and argued for yet more regulation. It did not seem to occur to them that regulation itself could be the cause of the weak price competition they had noticed.

A little thought indeed shows that the SEC's "inherent conflict" theory is deeply flawed. The relationship between the fund and the adviser is not a particularly unusual one. The fund is a buyer and the adviser is a seller. Our economy is composed of buyers and sellers. Whether we buy cell phone services, car repairs, or dry cleaning, we are always contracting with sellers of services who want to earn the highest possible profit from the transaction, while we, as buyers, want their services for the lowest cost consistent with the quality we desire. We do not normally think of this relationship as involving a conflict of interest, primarily because we know that competition keeps the prices of cell phone companies, auto repair shops, and dry cleaners within bounds. The fact that there are other sellers of the same services, with roughly the same quality, keeps all sellers from exploiting us.

If investment advisers were in fact competing with one another on price, any conflict of interest between the adviser and the fund—at least any conflict associated with the adviser's fees and expenses charged to the fund—would be irrelevant. The adviser would be compelled to lower its price as far as possible, in order to attract or retain investors, just as cell phone providers, auto repair shops, and dry cleaners must do. The fact that the fund cannot easily change advisers, as the Senate report noted, is largely irrelevant, because the investor can easily change funds. Yet for some reason the idea of an inherent conflict has transfixed the SEC, lawmakers, and academics for years. Instead, *the relevant issue is not the relationship between the adviser and the fund; it is why investment advisers do not compete on price as do all other service providers, in almost every other sector of the economy.*

By adopting a prescription that focuses on making the boards of directors of mutual funds more independent of the investment adviser, the SEC has not only focused debate on the wrong issue; it has also made the real problem worse by driving the industry even further from a competitive model. Accordingly, in our view, the way to address the lack of price competition in mutual funds is to abandon the current corporate structure and the role of the board in approving the investment adviser's fees and expenses. Instead, investment advisers should be permitted to set their own prices and to retain the benefits of lowering their costs in order to attract and retain more investors. In the resulting competition for investors, fees would fall as a matter of course as advisers seek new and more efficient ways to deliver their services. Moreover, once the board's role in price regulation is eliminated, a more effective system than a part-time board of directors can be put in place to address the conflicts of interest that may remain.

The new, noncorporate structure we recommend would be an option available to advisers and investors, not a mandatory substitute for existing mutual funds; it is outlined briefly below and discussed more fully in chapter 5.

Providing Collective Investment Services
through a Managed Investment Trust

Our proposal, in a nutshell, is that investment advisers be permitted to offer collective investment services to investors through a direct contractual relationship. Mutual funds organized under the current corporate form would remain in existence, and investors who are comfortable with this form of collective investment would continue to have access to it. However, to remove the existing barriers to price competition in the industry, we recommend that Congress authorize a new form of collective investment under the following alternative structure:

- Investment advisers would be authorized to offer collective investment services to the public for a single all-in fee covering all fees and expenses of the collective investment vehicle.

- As part of this service, the investment adviser would establish a trust at a bank that is independent of the adviser.

- The bank would maintain custody of the trust's cash and portfolio securities, issue trust units representing a beneficial interest in the trust in exchange for payment from investors, redeem units for cash at their NAV, and keep records of unit ownership.

- The bank would also hold title, as trustee, to the portfolio securities of the fund and would have a fiduciary duty to protect the interests of the unit holders, who are the beneficiaries of the trust.

This structure would be similar to the unit investment trust already authorized under the ICA. The difference is that the ICA unit investment trust is not managed; its portfolio remains fixed after the trust has been established. Accordingly, we call our proposed structure a "managed investment trust" (MIT). Under the MIT proposal, investors would be offered units in the trust, which would be registered like today's mutual funds under the Securities Act of 1933, rather than shares in a fund. Many provisions of the ICA would remain the same for MITs as for managed mutual funds. For example, each trust would be required to have a written investment policy describing how the adviser will invest its assets, and it would be forbidden to own more than a specified maximum percentage of the securities of any one issuer. The bank trustee would be responsible for ensuring that these restrictions are observed and for addressing other possible conflicts of interest, as we discuss in chapter 5.

Chapter 5 also proposes reforms—including reform of the tax laws governing investment income—that would make it easier for investors to move from one fund to another. This would further strengthen competition for investors' dollars.

One of the benefits of the MIT is that it would eliminate the tangible and intangible costs of a board of directors, including proxy solicitations, board salaries and travel, the preparation of cost analyses in connection with fee negotiations, and management time in tending to the other needs of the board. But this is not the reason we propose it. Our principal motivation is our view, outlined above, that rate regulation by a board of directors impairs the incentives of investment advisers to compete on price and thus keeps expense ratios of mutual funds higher than they would be in a fully competitive environment.

In this "market approach" to mutual fund regulation and policy, an investor would be treated much like a customer of any other financial service provider (or, for that matter, a purchaser of any other service or product). As usual in these relationships, the customer decides whether the quality of the service is worth the fee. We see nothing about a customer's relationship to a provider of collective investment services that sets it apart from other services transactions as far as setting fees is concerned. Indeed, investors contract every day with brokers and advisers who structure their portfolios for a fee, whether these are separately managed accounts or simply portfolios that develop out of individual recommendations of a broker or other adviser. In all these relationships, investors are thought to be perfectly capable of deciding whether the services they are receiving are worth the cost. No reason is readily apparent why a board of directors should be interposed between investor and adviser to make this determination when a collective investment is involved.[18]

Although we believe that competition will develop when investment advisers are free to set their own fees, some will certainly argue that this will be insufficient unless investors can be made to care about the costs imposed on their collective investments.[19] This argument, however, ignores much that microeconomists have learned about the sources of competitive pricing among firms. It is quite possible, even probable, that most investors will continue to be insensitive to costs, despite the fact that small differences in costs can be shown to have huge effects on investment success over the long term. But that is not what drives the market. The market is driven by the demands of the marginal investor. It is this investor—the last, careful, cost-conscious investor willing to pay more than the adviser's marginal cost—who will set the price for all others as investment advisers try to attract that investor by lowering the price for their services.

In a market where advisers are allowed to retain the profits that come from attracting these marginal investors, competition will arise, innovation and efficiency will increase, and prices will decline. This process has worked for brokerage commissions, air travel, trucking, and interstate telecommunications, to cite only a few of the markets where competition has demonstrated its superiority to regulation. We see no reason that it should not work for collective investments.

What Follows

Before we set out our proposed approach for facilitating competition in the collective investment industry, we attend to some preliminaries. In chapter 2 we describe briefly the evolution of the current regulatory approach, concluding with an analysis of why many want to see regulation reinforced or strengthened in light of the mutual fund scandals that surfaced earlier in this decade. Chapter 3 focuses on the remarkable growth of the mutual fund industry itself and on the growth of alternative asset diversification vehicles that are providing increased competition for funds.

In chapter 4 we take up the seeming paradox that stimulated this study: if the mutual fund industry is so competitive, why is there not more evidence of price competition, in the form of a narrower range of all-in costs? Here we lay out our claim that the utility-like regulatory regime that has long governed the industry is responsible. Here and in chapter 2, we also explain the limits of fund boards and why they failed to prevent the scandals that tarnished the industry several years ago.

The arguments in chapter 4 provide the rationale for the MIT proposal we outline in detail in chapter 5. Key to our proposal is the option to operate a collective investment vehicle without having a separate board of directors. Once boards are no longer involved in rate setting, the benefits they provide in the form of preventing conflicts of interest seem much less than their costs. As part-time watchdogs, with in some cases hundreds of funds to oversee, boards are not an efficient mechanism for finding or addressing conflicts of interest. Conflicts occur in every business and are usually effectively handled by competition and transparency. If a service provider is operating inefficiently because, for example, it is using an expensive affiliated company for some element of support, that provider will soon be driven out of business in a competitive market.

To the extent that competition is not a factor, boards are not likely to be particularly effective in preventing conflicts. A classic case in point is provided by the late-trading and market timing scandals of a few years ago. Those were actions of advisers alone and could never have come to the attention of boards. To address problems of this kind requires a full-time, professional staff, continuously in contact with the fund and aware of how it is being managed. We recommend such an arrangement for conflicts of interest in chapter 5. We draw on the U.K. system, which relies upon a "depository"—a trustee bank—charged with a fiduciary duty to act in the interest of shareholders.

It is time, in our view, for policymakers to stop trying to make part-time boards of directors into something they can never be, and to try something else. A look at the wide disparity in the costs of mutual funds shows that something is wrong. At bottom, the notion that boards can set "reasonable" fees for fund advisers conflicts with the bedrock economic principle—proven time and again in a market economy—that only competitive markets can produce the efficiencies that lead to low prices. There is no reason that the collective investment market, when advisers are free to set their own prices, should not become a price-competitive space.

All this does not mean that we recommend that policymakers immediately reject the regulatory mindset that has dominated mutual fund policy and regulation since the ICA was adopted. Rather, we urge in our concluding chapter that the Investment Company Act of 1940 simply be *supplemented* with provisions allowing fund organizers to use an alternative legal structure—the MIT rather than a separate corporation—as a way of delivering the collective investment services now delivered by mutual funds.

2

A Brief History of Mutual Fund Regulation:
The Conflict between the Required Structure of Investment Companies and the Economics of Collective Investment

Seven decades ago, the Nobel prize–winning economist Ronald Coase outlined the economic conditions under which it makes sense for firms to carry out multiple functions themselves rather than contract for them with third parties. When the savings in "transactions costs" from not having to negotiate, monitor, and enforce contracts outweigh any costs involved in internally managing a function and the people needed to perform it, he argued, the firm should perform that function internally.[1] The opposite is also true: services that are performed internally can be outsourced to more efficient suppliers when it is cheaper to do so. Changes in technology and economic institutions can tilt the balance in favor of outsourcing, often sharply. Cisco Systems, for example, one of the most successful suppliers of Internet switching equipment, and a publicly traded company with one of the largest market capitalizations on the New York Stock Exchange, has no manufacturing facilities of its own; it outsources all its manufacturing functions. An increasing number of U.S. companies have found it cheaper and more reliable to outsource various functions—like customer service, food supply, janitorial services, and other activities that are not central to their "core" operations—to service providers in the United States and elsewhere.

Economies of scale (possibly brought about by technological change) are one reason it might be less expensive to acquire certain services outside the firm. If economies of scale make it cheaper for a single company to perform a given service for a number of other firms than for each of those firms to perform the same service for itself, it makes economic sense for them to outsource that service to the single provider. Economies of scale probably provide the underlying economic reason why mutual funds have assumed their current structure, as entities that contract with outside providers of investment management and trading services. A mutual fund would have to be enormously large before it could sustain the cost of employing its own staff of investment analysts and traders; until it got to that size, its sponsors might have to endure many years of losses and missing paydays. However, if the analysts and traders form themselves into a single firm and offer their services to many funds on a contractual or outsourced basis, both they and the funds are more likely to prosper. This organizational form would be more efficient and would likely outcompete other forms, as long as a corporate form of organization was the only way that collective investment services could be provided. Thus the current structure of the mutual fund industry, in which "families" of funds are sponsored and managed by an investment adviser, may have been foreordained by the corporate structure that Congress prescribed for the investment company industry in the Investment Company Act of 1940.

Under the ICA, funds for all practical purposes may be organized in only one way. As the SEC staff noted in 1992, "Although the Act does not explicitly require that investment companies be organized in corporate form, it imposes requirements that assume the standard equipment of a corporate democracy: [including] a board of directors...whose function is to oversee the operations of the investment company and police conflicts of interest. . . ."[2] The act requires that each fund have its own portfolio and its own investment policies and offer its shares pursuant to its own SEC registration statement and prospectus. Although the act permits funds to be organized as either corporations or trusts, in both cases, in order to be recognized as managed investment companies (open- or closed-end), they have to be separate legal entities, each with a board of directors or a board of trustees. Once this structure was required, the laws of economics took over. If it was to grow at all, the industry had to develop into a vast number of individual funds, organized as corporations and grouped into families managed by outside organizations specializing in securities advisory services and trading.

In this chapter we trace the development of the mutual fund industry and show that the ICA dictates a structure for mutual funds that is inconsistent with the economics of collective investment management. We also show that the form specified by Congress is also inconsistent with the common law concept that a corporation must be managed by its board of directors. Together these factors account for both the industry's structure and the notion that there is a special conflict of interest—different from the normal conflicts between a buyer and seller—that characterizes the relationship between the investment adviser and the shareholders of the fund.

The Beginnings of the Mutual Fund Business—Until 1940

Investment companies can be viewed as an outgrowth of the securities industry, as that industry was fundamentally transformed by World War I. Faced with the need to finance that war, the federal government mounted a huge campaign to sell government "Liberty Bonds" to the public. This was the first time that millions of ordinary Americans placed some of their financial assets in securities rather than in banks, and it stimulated the development of a dynamic and sales-oriented securities industry. As the U.S. economy grew after the war, so did the industry, which helped to finance that growth through the sale of corporate equities and bonds in addition to government bonds. The emphasis in this early era of securities market development was on sales of securities rather than on managing money. Securities firms were always looking for products to sell to their customers rather than assets they could manage. By the mid-1920s, securities firms had found that, in addition to the shares of individual companies, investors had an appetite for buying ready-made baskets or portfolios of stocks. The virtues of asset diversification were known to the securities industry and were marketed to the wider public. Investment companies, then, got their start not as a means to manage money efficiently, but primarily as another product that securities firms and brokers could sell.[3]

The investment company was not an American invention. Corporations that pooled investors' money to buy shares of a number of companies had existed in Great Britain since the mid-1800s. The organizers of investment companies in the United States borrowed the concept from across the Atlantic.[4] However, the corporate form of investment company later disappeared in the United Kingdom. The fact that the corporate form remained dominant in the United States is the result of the ICA, which left no room for structural innovation by U.S. investment advisers. In Britain, with a less restrictive set of governing laws, the collective investment industry evolved into a more efficient form.

As noted in chapter 1, the first investment companies sold in the United States were organized as closed-end funds: corporations with portfolios of a fixed size and with a fixed number of shares outstanding. Investors could buy and sell the shares in the public markets, much as they bought and sold the shares of individual companies, but they could not go to the fund directly to redeem their shares for cash. Nevertheless, closed-end funds grew to become so popular that their shares sometimes sold at a premium: that is, at a price above the fund's NAV per share. By 1929 new investment companies were being formed at the rate of almost one per day.[5] The emphasis still, however, was on the distribution of shares—that was where the money was made—and not on the management of the investment company's portfolio. This is important, because the practice of structuring investment companies as separate corporations was established during this period, when distributing the shares of investment companies was a more important concern (and far more profitable) than managing the companies efficiently after the shares were placed.

Following the 1929 crash, the ability to redeem shares on demand, and so avoid outsized losses in an illiquid market, made open-end funds popular but also caused problems of its own. For example, because open-end funds were subject to a continuous flow of redemptions, they had to sell new shares continuously to maintain a given size, and thus they became entangled in the high-pressure sales tactics then permeating the industry.[6] Historically, open-end funds also tended to have different sponsors than closed-end funds. Whereas closed-end funds were sponsored primarily by investment bankers and brokers, who "distributed substantial blocks of securities within relatively short periods of time on the basis of their prestige and to an established clientele," the majority of open-end investment companies "were sponsored at some period of their existence by security salesmen or firms connected with the distribution of securities."[7] This latter group of sponsors "required no prestige, no clientele, and conducted continuous sales efforts with no definite ideas as to what the ultimate sizes of the investment companies would be."[8] Conveniently, these sales practices yielded consistent profits to management in the form of sales commissions, or loads.

A minority of open-end investment companies, however, were organized "primarily by fund managers and investment counsel, frequently as an adjunct to their established investment counsel business."[9] These companies derived their profits more from management fees than from sales loads, so an emphasis was placed on managing rather than selling. This, in turn, led to a "more intimate relationship between stockholders and sponsors . . . smaller investor turnover . . . and . . . average loading charges [that] were lower."[10] Yet because these companies were a minority, accounting for only about 22 percent of the open-end group's assets—and open-end funds themselves were a minor element of the industry at this time—they received little attention in the literature dealing with the investment company industry before the passage of the ICA. Instead, the focus in the SEC's 1939 report to Congress (discussed further below) was invariably on the abuses that took place in the larger group, namely, those "open-end investment companies sponsored by persons interested in distribution."[11]

Since both closed- and open-end companies were organized as corporations governed by boards of directors, they were fundamentally different from a third diversified investment vehicle, the "unit investment trust" (UIT), which enjoyed some popularity during the 1930s—but nothing approaching that of open-end funds. As the name implies, the assets of a UIT were held by a trustee rather than managed by a board or an outside investment adviser. Like a closed-end fund, the UIT had a fixed portfolio and was sold in units representing proportionate shares of the whole; however, like an open-end fund, these units could be redeemed for cash at the NAV per share. Unlike either closed- or open-end funds at that time, the UIT was not actively managed: it remained invested in the same portfolio throughout its life. A managed investment trust (or MIT), the entity we recommend in chapter 5 as an alternative to the mutual fund, would resemble a UIT, but its assets would be managed—that is, bought and sold as the manager perceives new opportunities for gain—and the trust could grow larger or smaller as new resources flowed in or investors redeemed their units for cash.

The 1929 stock market crash led to major changes in the legal landscape governing the equities markets—not surprisingly, given the severity of the losses that investors and the economy suffered. But first, investigations and hearings had to be convened and blame assessed. By 1934 Congress had enacted the fundamental pieces of legislation that govern the securities markets today. The SEC was established to oversee traders and trading, requiring that securities exchanges, brokers, and dealers register with the SEC and obligating public companies to disclose information about themselves, both when they issued stock and on a regular basis thereafter.

Congress waited somewhat longer to address concerns about investment companies, finally asking the SEC in 1936 for the report that was ultimately delivered in 1939. The report outlined many of the suspicions and allegations that had led to complaints about the industry before the onset of the Depression. These included outright looting of shareholders' funds, making speculative investments even when funds were marketed as conservative investments, and excessively leveraging (that is, borrowing against) fund assets. The SEC also found that some fund sponsors were steering the fund's brokerage business to their securities affiliates, and some of these engaged in churning (frequently trading securities in the portfolio so as to generate high brokerage fees). Other fund sponsors were found to have given preferential treatment to certain classes of shareholders, and others to have engaged in high-pressure sales tactics while awarding themselves excessive management fees.

The abuses were so widespread and so widely acknowledged that the mutual fund industry was ready to cooperate with the SEC to develop a solution, although it did not agree with all of the SEC's recommendations. By 1940 approximately 2 million Americans had placed at least some funds in investment companies, most of which were mutual funds. One out of every ten holders of securities of all types held them through an investment company, and most of these investors were of modest means. One quarter of all fund investors (in closed- and open-end funds combined) owned just ten shares or fewer, and well over half owned fifty or fewer.[12] If the industry wanted these investors to stick with their funds, change had to come.

The Investment Company Act of 1940

And so it did, in the form of the ICA, which the industry so strongly supported that it passed without a single dissenting vote in either house of Congress. The final bill embodied numerous changes from its initial version, however, which would have given the SEC much broader discretionary authority than it finally received. As one commentator put it at the time, "Where the original draft left the Commission with power by rule and regulation to implement the broad policies of the bill, the present Act generally sets certain maxima of regulation, leaving in the Commission a discretionary power only to exempt and minimize."[13]

Since the main problems identified by the SEC involved abuse of shareholders by funds' promoters and advisers, it is not surprising that Congress and the industry sought specific remedies for these, rather than a legal foundation on which the most efficient collective investment industry could evolve. The ICA addressed the industry as it was then, requiring all investment companies to register with the SEC and placing many specific statutory restrictions on what funds would be permitted to do. A surprisingly large number of ICA provisions begin with the words "It shall be unlawful for any registered investment company. . . ." At the same time, the ICA authorized the SEC to exempt "any person, entity or transaction from any provision of the Act, provided the exemption is necessary and consistent with the protection of investors." The SEC's later administration of the act— particularly its efforts to enhance the proportion and powers of independent directors—has consisted largely of an imaginative use of this broad exemption authority. Initially, the ICA required that:

- at least 40 percent of fund boards be made up of "disinterested" or "independent" members—persons with no financial interest or employment relationship with the investment adviser;

- funds have written contracts with their investment advisers and with the underwriters of their shares, approved by the independent directors and the holders of a majority of shares outstanding, spelling out the nature of the adviser's and the underwriter's compensation, and capable of being terminated at any time by the board or shareholders;

- funds disclose their investment policies, also subject to shareholder approval, and whether the fund was to be diversified or not;

- funds refrain from engaging in principal transactions with affiliates, although affiliates could act as fund brokers; and

- funds file reports with the SEC at least twice a year (now quarterly), detailing, among other things, their holdings, purchases, and sales of securities.

The specific powers of the board of directors outlined in the ICA, beyond approving the advisory and underwriting contracts, were relatively few. The independent directors were to select independent public accountants as auditors, oversee permissible transactions with affiliates, and review and approve fidelity bonds. The full board was to estimate the value of certain types of securities in the portfolio, approve custody agreements for the fund's portfolio securities, and make judgments as to credit quality for major investments in fixed-income securities.

The convoluted structure that the ICA cemented into place put investment advisers and fund boards of directors in opposition to one another. Viewed from the perspective of the board of directors—and eventually that of the SEC—the adviser's effort to profit from its services conflicted with the interests of the shareholders whom the directors were supposed to protect. However, viewed from the perspective of the adviser, the ICA required not only the creation of a separate corporate entity in order to offer collective investment services but also a great deal of investment to get it established as a going concern. For the risks and costs involved, the adviser should expect to profit.

As outlined in chapter 1, this is a needless conflict, created entirely by the ICA's requirement that collective investment vehicles in the United States be organized in corporate form. The "inherent conflict" cited by the SEC and critics of the mutual fund industry, at least as far as fee-setting is concerned, is nothing more than the usual divergence of interests between a buyer and a seller, but when it arises in the context of a corporation's relationship with a supplier of services, it assumes a different cast. In other sectors of the economy, this divergence of interests between a buyer and seller is not treated as a problem. For example, if a fund investor wants to establish a separately managed account that contains all the same stocks that the fund contains, and in the same proportions, he or she can do so simply by contracting with an investment adviser. If dissatisfied with that adviser's service, or the price for that service, the investor can change to another adviser. If the adviser, in assembling the portfolio, uses affiliated brokerage services that are more expensive than necessary, the investor may decide to cease using that adviser, or may decide that other aspects of the adviser's services are still worth the price and continue to use them. But few investors will think of the adviser's use of an expensive affiliated broker as a conflict of interest. To most investors, the adviser's choice of a broker is just one more element of the costs associated with the adviser's services, and the only question is whether the service, overall, is worth the cost.

To be sure, a mutual fund's board of directors, unlike an individual investor, cannot easily move the fund's business from one adviser to another if it is dissatisfied with the adviser's services. There are several good reasons for this. First, it is the shareholders of the fund, not the directors, who actually chose the adviser by investing in the fund. With all due respect to fund boards, they are not the reason that investors buy shares in a given fund. Under these circumstances, the board would have to have very good reasons for countermanding what appears to have been a considered decision of the fund's shareholders to buy and hold shares of the fund. In addition, in order to create the fund, the adviser will have incurred substantial costs, and reasonably expects to recover those costs along with a profit. If directors regularly exercised their authority to terminate advisory contracts, there would be no incentive for advisers to create new funds.

But this focus on the relationship between the board and the adviser is illusory. Even if the board cannot easily change advisers, fund shareholders can and do move their investments from one fund to another with relative ease. The fund families involved in the late-trading and market timing scandals in 2003 suffered substantial losses, as shareholders redeemed their shares and went elsewhere.[14] Similarly, fund shareholders have shown a marked preference for no-load funds rather than funds with front-end or back-end loads,[15] and the funds that have been growing fastest over the last five years are those with the lowest expense ratios.[16] Finally, and most important, the most significant supposed conflicts of interest—those involving the adviser's fees and expenses—would be eliminated if investment advisers were to compete on price. This would force advisers to seek more efficient and innovative ways of providing their collective investment services, and—as in all other areas of the economy where competition exists—there would be no need for a board of directors to force them to reduce their fees as their costs decline.

All of this, however, goes back to one simple point: the ICA sets up a structure for collective investment that is inconsistent with the industry's economics. There would be no recognizable conflict of interest in the relationship between adviser and fund shareholder if the shareholder chose the adviser directly, instead of having to acquire the adviser's services through investing in a corporation. Without the interposition of a corporation, investors in a collective investment vehicle such as an MIT would view their relationship with the adviser as similar to that with a securities broker or any other supplier of services. The cost would be matched against the quality of the services on offer. This would certainly be true of the marginal investors that investment advisers would be trying to reach through lowering their management fees and associated costs, but all investors would be more conscious of the costs associated with their investment if they viewed the transaction as a purchase of services rather than an investment in shares. As we elaborate more fully in chapter 4, by eliminating the requirement for board approval of the adviser's pricing, and allowing advisers to keep the profits they earn from attracting larger numbers of investors (eliminating, in other words, fee breakpoints based on supposed economies of scale), the obstacles that now inhibit price competition among investment advisers would be lifted.

Post-1940 Refinements

With the end of World War II and the recovery of the stock market, investment companies—open-end funds in particular—began to grow in popularity. As they did, legal analysts and observers expressed concern that the ICA did not go far enough to ensure that management contracts between the fund and its investment adviser were truly negotiated at arm's length. Accordingly, in the 1960s Congress requested two studies of the fund industry: one by scholars at the University of Pennsylvania's Wharton School of Business, completed in 1962, and the other (which drew heavily on the Wharton report) by SEC staff, published in 1966.[17] Both, failing to see the forest for the trees, focused primarily on the relationship between the investment adviser and the fund, and this marked the beginning of the SEC view—outlined in chapters 1 and 4—that the key to reducing fund costs was to empower the independent directors in their negotiations with investment advisers.

The Wharton report added that fund boards lacked bargaining power in dealing with the adviser who created the fund, and it expressed little faith that investors or even the independent directors could control the adviser. Indeed, the Wharton report questioned the independence of the "independent" directors, since they typically were chosen by individuals affiliated with the adviser. This conclusion was reinforced by the SEC's finding that a fund's board could not easily terminate its relationship with the adviser. The SEC study further concluded, among other things, that despite the growth of the fund industry, competition among funds was too weak to force any lowering of fees. As evidence, the SEC study noted that 43 percent of fund assets were concentrated under the management of the top five advisers.

Together these complaints implied that fund expense ratios were higher than necessary because investment advisers were overcharging fund shareholders for their services. This was especially true, it was suggested, as funds increased in size; economies of scale should have led to lower fees as a percentage of fund assets, but frequently did not. In addition, the SEC report concluded that the legal standard for challenging the reasonableness of advisers' contracts in court—one that required proof of "corporate waste"—was too narrow to be effective in reining in fees.

The Wharton and SEC reports, along with other criticisms of the industry and the ICA, led Congress in 1970 to amend the act in several ways. The amendments strengthened the independence requirement for board members, tightening the act's definition of independence. The amendments added a new section 36(b), which explicitly imposed a fiduciary duty on investment advisers in seeking compensation from the fund, and both the SEC and shareholders were given rights to enforce this obligation. Although the Senate committee that drafted the amendments specifically stated that it did not intend by this provision to impose a "cost-plus" system for board fee regulation, judicial interpretation—as discussed in chapter 4—subsequently turned fee setting into precisely that. Congress did not directly address sales loads, but instead left in place the preexisting system of SEC oversight to prevent charges that were "unconscionable."

The one consistent element in the SEC's policies after its 1966 report was the use of its statutory authority to increase the number of independent directors on fund boards and to enhance their authority to challenge the investment adviser. In 1971, in the case of *Rosenfeld v. Black*, the U.S. Court of Appeals for the Second Circuit ruled that an adviser to a closed-end fund was in violation of its fiduciary duty when it sold the fund's advisory contract to another adviser. The court held that because the contract was an asset of the fund, the adviser was not entitled to sell it. This decision resulted in a great deal of uncertainty for advisers, since selling the stock of the advisory firm to a successor adviser had been a traditional means of capturing the value of a business that had been built up over many years. At the urging of the SEC, in 1975 Congress again amended the ICA to permit mutual fund advisers to sell their advisory contracts provided two conditions were met: first, that at least 75 percent of the board members were independent for at least three years following the transaction; and second, that the transaction did not impose any unfair burden on the fund.[18] This was the first effort by the SEC to increase the percentage of independent directors on fund boards, and it arose in special circumstances. Subsequent efforts were to be linked to exemptions from the ICA that were requested by the mutual fund industry.

For example, in 1980 the SEC permitted an exemption from the ICA for a fund that wanted to use fund assets to pay for share distributions under section 12(b) of the ICA. The exemption was granted on condition that the board of the fund be composed of a majority of independent directors, and those directors were to select and nominate all new independent directors.[19]

The SEC went a step further in 1992, with the release of a study by its Division of Investment Management titled *Protecting Investors: A Half Century of Investment Company Regulation*. In this study the Division recommended that all boards have a majority of independent directors, arguing that this was necessary for the independent directors as a group to carry out their oversight responsibilities effectively.[20] Thereafter the SEC moved purposefully to ensure that independent directors formed a majority of all fund boards.

Thus, although the ICA's original language requiring only 40 percent of a fund's directors to be independent is still on the books, the Commission has virtually eliminated it by regulation. In particular, in 2001 the Commission issued a rule requiring all funds to have board majorities of independent directors if they wanted to make use of certain important exemptions from the act.[21] According to the final rule release, this requirement would enable the independent directors to have "a more meaningful influence on fund management and represent shareholders from a position of strength."[22] This ruling also required that funds making use of these exemptions have arrangements under which their independent directors selected and nominated other independent directors, and that any legal counsel for a fund's independent directors also be independent of the adviser (although there is no requirement to hire counsel).

Three years after its rule requiring an independent majority of directors, in the wake of the late-trading and market timing scandals discussed below, the SEC issued another rule on fund governance, effectively raising the minimum share of independent directors to 75 percent and requiring that all boards have an independent chair. Because it lacked specific authority to do so, the Commission did not impose the new requirements directly, but instead tied them to a fund's use of any of ten important exemptive rules. In the final rule release, the Commission argued that, in light of the scandals, "the 2001 amendments do not go far enough in addressing the need for independent fund boards," and that greater independence was necessary in order for the board to manage conflicts of interest between the adviser and the fund.[23] However, in April 2006 the D.C. Circuit Court of Appeals struck down the rule on the grounds that the Commission had "failed to perform its statutory duty to consider efficiency, competition, and capital formation in connection with this rule-making."[24]

Ironically, the SEC has not always been tied to the ICA structure. In 1982, in the midst of the Reagan administration's efforts to foster deregulation, the SEC issued a "concept paper" in which it outlined a wholly different system of mutual fund investment, one that would dispense with the corporate form and allow funds to be organized as managed unitary investment funds (UIFs).[25] In this the SEC adapted an idea advanced in 1980 by securities lawyer Stephen K. West. The UIF, organized as a trust, would hold the fund's assets but have neither shareholders nor directors. Instead the SEC would supervise the trust, presumably guarding against excessive fee arrangements and possible conflicts involving the investment adviser. We revisit West's UIF proposal in chapter 4.

Apart from the general push toward deregulation in the Reagan administration, the SEC's UIF concept seems to have been prompted by two important changes in the fund industry after the 1970 amendments.[26] The first was what appeared to be an investor preference for no-load funds. This was a clear case of investors putting downward market pressure on a fee that they were required to pay directly, rather than indirectly through the fund. The second was the rapid growth of money market funds (MMFs), a result of controls on the interest rates that could be paid on bank deposits. In the late 1970s and early 1980s, when inflation soared into double digits, so did the returns on U.S. Treasury securities. Because annual interest rates on bank deposits were limited to 5 percent, depositors began to move large sums from bank deposits to MMFs, which were invested in Treasury securities, jumbo certificates of deposit, and commercial paper, all of which were unregulated and paid substantially higher rates than bank deposits.

Because shares in MMFs were denominated "at par" (that is, at a fixed NAV of $1.00 per share), they could be redeemed with no capital gains tax consequences. This meant that investors could easily move from one fund to another simply by selling their shares, whereas redemptions from the typical equity or bond fund often triggered capital gains tax obligations. The prevalence of MMFs in the mutual fund industry at that time gave it an aura of competitiveness, which may have induced the SEC to consider a new structure in which competitive pricing by advisers would supplant price regulation by fund boards. In addition, the SEC's concept paper pointed out that the process of board of directors voting was costly and that it was unclear whether the benefits of board of directors oversight (as weak as it was) outweighed the costs.

But the SEC's interest in the UIF concept was short-lived. The Commission seemed to be concerned that investors did not focus sufficiently on fees, but instead only on a fund's performance, and could not be relied upon to discipline fee setting by advisers. We believe this was a mistake. As we discuss in chapter 4, the SEC should have recognized that fee setting by the board of directors impairs the ability of investment advisers to compete, and thus their incentive to find ways to lower their fees. The competition that developed among advisers to create no-load funds should have been seen by the SEC as an indication that investors were capable of disciplining advisers on fees when they realized that a fee—in this case a sales load—came directly out of their pockets.

The Mutual Fund Scandals of 2003 and Their Aftermath

In establishing funds as corporate vehicles, the ICA intended fund boards not only to oversee the advisory fees paid to investment managers but also to prevent managers from engaging in the kinds of abuses that had led Congress to enact the ICA in the first place. The highly publicized late-trading and market timing scandals earlier in this decade provided an opportunity for the SEC to increase the independence of fund boards, even though this remedy was inapposite for the problem it was intended to address. In fact, the late-trading and market timing scandals had nothing to do with the existence or absence of board independence, because the scandals stemmed from decisions by investment advisers that would never have come to a board's attention. This in itself reveals the deficiencies of a board as a monitoring device. Boards, which meet quarterly or at most monthly, are simply not equipped to discover anything about the adviser's activities that the adviser does not choose to tell them. But before we discuss this point in detail, it is useful to summarize the scandals briefly.

The story effectively begins in September 2003, when New York State Attorney General Eliot Spitzer rocked the mutual fund industry by filing a two-pronged complaint against Canary Capital Partners, a hedge fund, which implicated various mutual funds in two separate (but related) sets of improper practices. The investigation and the two elements of the Canary case attracted a flurry of media attention at the time and for months afterward. The scandal eventually widened to include other parties and was later picked up by the SEC.

One of the complaints lodged against Canary was that certain mutual funds had allowed it to engage in "late-trading." Also called after-hours trading, this practice involved the purchase or sale of fund shares after 4 p.m. Eastern time, when the NAVs for all funds are calculated. The price for these transactions would be the 4 p.m. closing NAV, even though all transactions after 4 p.m. are supposed to be effected at the following day's price. As Attorney General Spitzer observed, this was like betting on yesterday's horse race. By buying or selling at a price set ahead of the next day's opening, an astute trader equipped with information that would affect the next day's trading (the announcement that Apple was going to release its iPod, for example) could essentially lock in a profit risk-free.

In fact, the law had already anticipated this kind of arbitrage, and it had been banned at least since 1968. Late-trading not only gives certain investors an unfair advantage, but also enables traders to earn arbitrage profits directly at the expense of the mutual fund, thus imposing losses on other shareholders by diluting the value of their holdings.[27]

Spitzer's other allegation accused Canary and its mutual fund adviser partners of engaging in "market timing." Unlike late-trading, market timing is not specifically illegal, and indeed professional traders have engaged in the practice since at least the 1920s. Market timing, as the term is generally used,[28] involves buying fund shares at a price that is "stale" (old) because of differences in time zones and then redeeming the shares at a profit once the price catches up. This occurs often (but not always) with respect to funds that concentrate in stocks listed on foreign exchanges.

Like late-trading, market timing dilutes the profits available for other, longer-term fund investors. Fund managers may have to keep larger amounts of cash on hand to meet the redemption demands of market timers, and their frequent trades lead to higher brokerage and administrative costs. Despite the technical legality of the practice, Attorney General Spitzer found an indirect way to address it, by bringing his cases against the funds under a provision of New York State's Martin Act, which authorizes the attorney general to seek monetary and equitable relief against those who engage in fraud in the offer or sale of securities. Spitzer charged the funds that had assisted Canary (and other market timers) with false disclosures: they had claimed in their prospectuses that they diligently inhibited market timing when in fact they did not.[29]

One natural question arises from the late-trading and market timing cases: why did the fund managers go along with the practice when it was their customers, rather than they themselves, who profited directly from the arbitrage? The answer, according to the New York State complaint, was that, in the wake of the stock market collapse after April 2000, when many customers began pulling money out of their funds, the targeted mutual funds permitted late-trading and market timing in exchange for an agreement by the customers to park substantial investments with other funds in the same fund family. These parked funds, in turn, increased the advisers' compensation.

Spitzer and other attorney generals in other states who launched similar investigations against a wide range of parties ultimately settled with all of their targets. Under the typical settlement, the traders disgorged their profits, and the mutual fund companies with which they had done business agreed to penalties, and often to lower their fees. Indirectly, then, the attorney generals used the late-trading and market timing charges to impose company-specific fee controls—something which, although technically out of their purview, can be loosely viewed as a way of providing restitution to current shareholders. (We say "loosely" because the agreements to lower fees also benefit new fund purchasers, who never would have suffered harm from the late-trading or market timing.[30])

In contrast, in one of the leading late-trading cases it pursued (against Alliance Capital Management), the SEC did not seek fee cuts, but instead insisted upon a truly independent chair of the fund's board. (In the end, Alliance reached a separate settlement with New York State in which it agreed to lower its fees by 20 percent.) Indeed, then-SEC Chairman William Donaldson argued that it was inappropriate for authorities to "piggyback" fee-cut settlements on the unrelated late-trading and market timing charges.[31]

As noted above, the SEC reacted to the scandals by adopting a rule that required 75 percent of mutual fund board members, and the fund's chair, to be independent of the adviser. This rule was twice overturned by the D.C. Court of Appeals. In mid-2006, under a new SEC chairman, Christopher Cox, who had not participated in the adoption of the earlier rule, the Commission sought comment on whether it should again adopt the rule. As of this writing, the SEC has taken no steps to do so.

The Commission's reaction to the late-trading and market timing scandals is consistent with its long-held view—most likely shared by the Commission's congressional overseers—that an independent board is the investor's best protection against unscrupulous activity, whether engaged in directly by investment advisers or simply facilitated by them (as in the case of late-trading or market timing). But, as we argue in more detail in subsequent chapters, there is little logic to support this view.

For example, in the case of late-trading, such practices have been illegal for over three decades. In other realms of activity—whether it be compliance with the antitrust, tax, or civil rights laws—policymakers do not assume that boards of directors are able to stop or root out such activities. At most, they can insist that managers have appropriate compliance officers and procedures in place to ensure that employees behave properly. But this is a weak substitute for control over advisers. If an advisory firm's management wants to participate in late-trading or market timing arrangements with favored customers, or in any other fraudulent or improper activity, it will hide these activities from compliance officers just as it has hidden them from boards. Adding more independent directors to boards will neither change this fact nor increase the likelihood that directors will be able to prevent illegal or improper activities by advisers. Indeed, making boards even more independent of and distant from advisers is likely to reduce the chances that such activities will be discovered.

Some have claimed nonetheless that vigilant boards could have prevented late-trading, or at least deterred it, by insisting that management provide them with fund turnover data.[32] Presumably, they argue, an increase in turnover could have signaled the presence of arbitrage. This seems highly unlikely. In many fund groups, directors oversee as many as 50 or 100 funds. The likelihood is small that they would have time to check turnover numbers for all these funds and detect unexpected increases. In reality, it seems that the SEC used the late-trading and market timing scandals as a way to pursue its long-term goal of increasing the independence of fund boards vis-à-vis their advisers.

Thus the SEC's effort to increase board independence after the scandals highlights both the agency's long-term effort to empower independent directors and the inability of such directors—or boards—to prevent improper activities involving the investment adviser. This, in turn, provides a clear example of the SEC's failure to understand and act upon the real source of the problems of the mutual fund industry. Mesmerized by the idea of an "inherent conflict of interest" between advisers and fund shareholders, the SEC has pursued a failed strategy for more than forty years. By attempting to increase the independence of boards from investment advisers, it has impaired the ability of the mutual fund industry to perform its principal mission as the low-cost collective investment vehicle for the great American middle class. Continuing this policy in the future is likely also to impair the industry's ability to hold its own in competition with the other, newer collective investment vehicles that we discuss in the next chapter.

3

The Growth of the Mutual Fund Industry and Its Competitors

The U.S. mutual fund industry now controls over $10 trillion in assets, more than all the deposits managed by banks,[1] and more than is held in individual stocks.[2] What began as an investment product for the Boston elite back in the 1920s has since opened America's financial markets to all. Mutual funds were instrumental in more than doubling the prevalence of equity ownership in the United States in just over twenty years, from 19 percent of households in 1983 to over 50 percent in 2005.[3] Moreover, with the increasing costs of higher education, the decline of defined-benefit pension plans, and the increased duration of the average retirement, Americans today must invest more in order to meet their family obligations and provide responsibly for their own nonworking years.

Happily, as the demand for investment vehicles has increased, the market has responded with a proliferation of new means of asset diversification. Over the past several years especially, not only have mutual fund companies vastly expanded their product selection, but alternative investment vehicles such as hedge funds, exchange-traded funds, and separately managed accounts have emerged as competitors to traditional mutual funds. Investors will benefit from this increased competition, but it will be a challenge for the fund industry.

This chapter will describe the growth of the collective investment business and the increasing competition between mutual funds and the newer asset diversification vehicles that a vigorous market has spawned. Of all these competing collective investment media, however, mutual funds remain the simplest way to achieve asset diversification and should in theory be the least expensive. The fact that they often are not has important public policy implications.

The Postwar Boom in Mutual Funds

The collective investment industry, and open-end funds in particular, mush-roomed after the end of World War II. According to the Investment Company Institute (ICI), in 1940 total assets of the industry stood at $450 million. Forty years later they had risen to $135 billion. By 1990 assets had crossed the $1 trillion mark, and in the fall of 2006 mutual fund assets exceeded $10 trillion (figure 3-1). In short, over a span of roughly sixty-six years, assets in mutual funds multiplied by an extraordinary 2,000-fold in nominal terms.[4]

FIGURE 3-1
NET ASSETS OF ALL U.S. MUTUAL FUNDS
(Trillions of dollars)

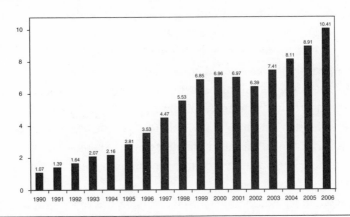

SOURCE: ICI, *2006 Investment Company Fact Book*, 71, and "Trends in Mutual Fund Investing, December 2006," http://www.ici.org/stats/latest/trends_12_06.html (accessed February 16, 2007). NOTE: Figure includes equity, bond, hybrid, and money market funds.

Several factors account for this meteoric rise. First, nominal stock market returns (including reinvested dividends) over the postwar period have averaged roughly 10 percent a year, doubling (before inflation) the assets in a well-diversified portfolio every seven years.[5] This rate of growth can account for a roughly 100-fold increase in mutual fund industry assets—a lot, to be sure, but well below the spectacular rise in the industry's assets under management.

Other factors were also at work. Although the Securities Act of 1933 and the Securities Exchange Act of 1934 were both based on the notion that individuals could do a good job of picking stocks if given sufficient information, studies by economists and other financial specialists repeatedly questioned whether anyone—even professionals—could improve upon the returns offered over the long term by the market as a whole. This idea seemed to seep into the public consciousness. Similarly, economists and investment advisers repeatedly emphasized that the risks of investing could be substantially reduced through diversification—buying many different stocks and even distributing investments among other asset classes such as bonds and real estate. Thus, as America got richer over the postwar period, millions of Americans sought asset diversification, apparently recognizing that the best way to diversify was to engage specialists—the managers of mutual funds—rather than do it on their own.

One of the most important forces driving the growth of the fund industry was the creation by Congress of tax-favored defined-contribution pension plans, first in the form of Individual Retirement Accounts (IRAs) in 1974 (as part of the legislation that established a broad framework for pension plans generally, the Employment Retirement Income Security Act, or ERISA), and later in the form of the plan outlined in section 401(k) of the Internal Revenue Code in 1978.[6] As figure 3-2 shows, by year-end 2005 nearly 40 percent of all mutual fund assets were in some form of retirement plan, and these in turn amounted to $3.4 trillion out of $14.3 trillion in all retirement fund assets.

Meanwhile the fund industry itself diversified, as different fund families began multiplying the choices they made available to investors. Initially, funds fell into two very broad classes, bond funds and equity funds. But as has often happened with other products (the magazine industry comes to mind), fund managers soon realized that different investors had different tastes and different investment objectives. Some wanted only particular kinds of equities, such as those that targeted specific industries or, later, specific parts of the world (including globally diversified funds). Others wanted different types of bonds, from those issued by the U.S. government, or by state and local governments (returns on which generally were not taxable), or by corporations, to those backed by assets (such as mortgages), to those issued by foreign borrowers. Bond funds also specialized in bonds of

FIGURE 3-2

SHARE OF U.S. MUTUAL FUND ASSETS HELD IN RETIREMENT PLANS

(Percent)

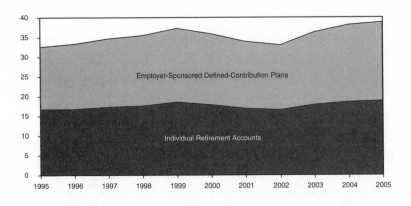

SOURCE: ICI, *2006 Investment Company Fact Book*, 58.

different maturities. Together these different funds gave investors a choice as to returns and the risks they were willing to bear.

The proliferation of funds of different types, combined with the huge impetus provided by tax-advantaged savings arrangements, caused mutual fund investment to soar. As figure 3-3 on the following page shows, except for the short-term decline between 2000 and 2003—coincident with both the decline in the securities market generally and the late-trading and market timing scandals—mutual funds of various types have grown rapidly since the early 1990s.

Figure 3-3 also highlights two innovations over the past three decades that are particularly worth mentioning. First, as discussed in the previous chapter, the combination of soaring market interest rates on Treasury securities in the late 1970s and early 1980s, coupled with mandated interest rate ceilings on bank and thrift deposits, led to the explosive growth of money market funds. MMFs invested primarily in short-term Treasury securities, along with highly rated commercial paper (short-term debt issued by corporations, typically secured by a standby guarantee or line of credit from a bank), and thus could offer interest rates well above those offered by banks and thrifts at the time. In the short span of three years, from 1979 to 1982, assets in MMFs grew from $46 billion to $220 billion.

FIGURE 3-3

NET ASSETS OF U.S. MUTUAL FUNDS BY FUND TYPE

(Trillions of dollars)

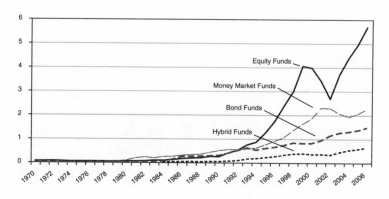

SOURCE: ICI, *2006 Investment Company Fact Book*, 73 and "Trends in Mutual Fund Investing, December 2006," http://www.ici.org/stats/latest/trends_12_06.html (accessed February 16, 2007).

But the growth of MMFs continued even after Congress deregulated bank deposit interest rates in the early 1980s. Investors apparently became accustomed to this new investment vehicle and continued to add funds to it. No doubt a major reason is that, despite the fact that MMFs are not seen as backed by a federal guarantee, no MMF has ever "broken the buck"; that is, none has ever let its share price fall below the $1 price at which they are offered. Indeed, on a few occasions the sponsors of these funds have felt it necessary to absorb principal losses in order to redeem shares at the $1 price.

The second important innovation was the index fund, whose development and growth date intellectually from the pioneering book on stock market investing, *A Random Walk Down Wall Street*, by Princeton's Burton Malkiel, first published in 1973.[7] Among Malkiel's principal arguments was that most investors would be far better off investing in the market as a whole, as represented by a broad index, than by attempting to select individual stocks. Vanguard was the first mutual fund family to respond to this observation, creating the Vanguard S&P 500 Index fund in 1976. The company has since created a number of funds based on other indexes, and many other funds have done the same. As will be discussed shortly, an entirely new financial instrument, the exchange-traded fund or ETF, is

FIGURE 3-4
NET ASSETS OF U.S. INDEX FUNDS
(Billions of dollars)

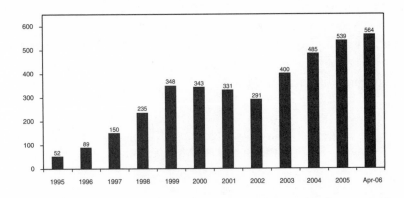

SOURCE: Financial Research Corporation, unpublished data.

based in part on the indexing concept. Figure 3-4 illustrates the rapid growth of assets in index mutual funds, which, like that of the fund industry as a whole, was interrupted by the decline in overall stock prices from 2000 to 2002 but has since resumed, although at a slower pace.

One of the more recent innovations in the fund industry is the "hybrid" fund, which invests in a combination of equity, debt, and other financial instruments. According to ICI data, in late 2006 there were 512 such funds with total net assets of $633 billion—more than are held in index funds. Hybrid funds come in three broad types. In "asset allocation" funds, the investment adviser shifts the fund's holdings across asset classes, depending on its view of which classes are likely to perform best over some horizon. "Lifestyle" funds allocate their holdings across asset classes to achieve a particular degree of risk (such as aggressive, moderate, or conservative). "Lifecycle" funds change the asset mix of the individual investor's portfolio over time, moving toward safer (bond or other fixed-income) investments as the investor approaches and then enters retirement. Lifecycle funds increasingly are becoming the default option for retirement funds. Both lifecycle and lifestyle funds have expanded rapidly in recent years, reaching $70 billion and $97 billion in assets, respectively, at year-end 2005, from essentially nothing ten years before.[8]

It is not only the diversity of funds that has expanded, but also their sheer number. Figure 3-5 shows that between 1940 and 1984, the number of funds grew somewhat slowly but remained under 1,000. From 1984 until 2002, in contrast, the number of funds climbed at a rapid pace, reaching over 8,000, but it has remained relatively steady since then. Of course, many of the new funds are created within existing fund families. Nonetheless, the explosion in the number of funds clearly indicates that investors have much more choice among funds than they had twenty years ago.

FIGURE 3-5
NUMBER OF U.S. MUTUAL FUNDS
(Thousands)

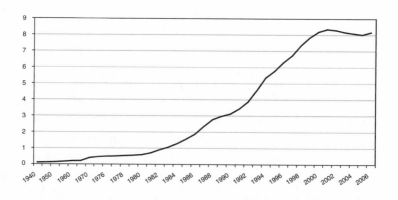

SOURCE: ICI, *2006 Investment Company Fact Book*, 71 and "Trends in Mutual Fund Investing, December 2006," http://www.ici.org/stats/latest/trends_12_06.html (accessed February 16, 2007). NOTE: Figure includes equity, bond, hybrid, and money market funds.

Who Owns Mutual Funds?

The growing popularity of mutual funds is reflected not just in the volume of assets held by the industry, or even in the proliferation of types and numbers of funds. Perhaps the best indicator is the share of U.S. households that have at least some assets invested in mutual funds. By this standard the growth of mutual funds has also been explosive: in 1980 this share was just 5.7 percent, but by 2005 it stood at 47.5 percent, a roughly eightfold increase. The later figure translates into some 91 million investors and 54 million households.[9]

Mutual funds also reflect the democratization of stock ownership in this country. Funds are no longer just for the rich, as they were when first formed in the 1920s. By 2005 nearly half of all families earning between $35,000 and $50,000 owned mutual fund shares, and ownership was at 70 percent among households with earnings above $50,000.[10]

Competition in and for the Fund Industry

The critical issue for policymakers, and the question behind this study, is why the fund industry, which appears to be competitively structured, shows signs of oligopoly—or, as the GAO phrased it in its 2000 report, "monopolistic competition."[11] Both the Wharton study of 1962 and the SEC study of 1966 noticed this phenomenon and advanced theories to explain it. As noted in chapters 1 and 2, we think these theories are wrong, and that the steps adopted on the basis of these theories by Congress and the SEC since 1962 have been misplaced. Chapter 4 outlines our view of why this competitively structured industry shows evidence of weak price competition, but first, in this chapter, it is useful to look more carefully at the structure of the mutual fund industry and the other collective investment vehicles with which it competes.

Table 3-1 depicts the market shares held by the top five, ten, and twenty-five mutual fund families by total assets in the United States since 1985. The combined market share of the top five families did not change

TABLE 3-1
ASSETS OF LARGEST FUND FAMILIES AS SHARE OF
TOTAL U.S. FUND ASSETS, SELECTED YEARS (Percent)

Fund Families	1985	1990	1995	2000	2005
Five largest	37	34	34	32	37
Ten largest	54	53	47	46	48
Twenty-five largest	78	75	70	74	71

SOURCE: ICI, *2006 Investment Company Fact Book*, 13.

between 1985 and 2005, remaining at 37 percent, but that level of industry concentration is low by any reasonable standard. Indeed, even the combined share of the top ten families, which once accounted for a bit more
than half of industry-wide assets, was down to less than 50 percent by
2005. Meanwhile the combined share of the top twenty-five families has
also fallen consistently, but more sharply, from near 80 percent to 71 percent. All these market shares are low in comparison with other industries
such as automobiles, steel, and many consumer goods.

Any doubt about this conclusion should be put to rest by the measure
for industry concentration most favored by the federal antitrust authorities:
the Herfindahl-Hirschman index (HHI). This index is calculated by sum-
ming the squares of the market shares of individual firms and multiplying
by 100, thus taking into account both the number and the relative size of
firms in the industry. The antitrust authorities consider any market in
which the HHI is above 1,800 to be concentrated; a market with an HHI
between 1,000 and 1,800 to be moderately concentrated; and an industry
with an HHI below 1,000 to be unconcentrated. The authorities use these
markers primarily to determine how intensely to scrutinize proposed mergers between companies in a given industry, and where to focus their
resources for investigating market abuses (with concentrated industries
receiving the most attention, understandably).

In 2005 the HHI for the mutual fund industry stood at around 400, or
well within the unconcentrated category.[12] In plain English, this means that
the industry is highly competitive. If anyone ever thought the fund market
was too concentrated for investors to have a meaningful choice among fund
families, and thus to exert market discipline against excessive fees, this sta-
tistic and the figures above clearly rebut that view. According to the standard commonly used by the federal antitrust agencies, the mutual fund
industry should be one of the most competitive in the country.

Furthermore, investors act as though the industry is competitive. They do
not always stick with one fund family forever, but instead take advantage of the
choices among funds, and between funds and other investment vehicles,
including direct asset ownership. Figure 3-6 illustrates, in each year since 1990,
the percentage of long-term funds that experienced net outflows that year, primarily because of investors taking out all or a portion of their investments. That
share has ranged between 24 and 48 percent. This continued movement of

investments *out* of these funds indicates that, despite any transactions costs (including redemption fees charged by funds and the potential triggering of capital gains taxes that some redemptions entail), fund investors will move.

FIGURE 3-6
SHARE OF U.S. MUTUAL FUND FAMILIES WITH NET CASH OUTFLOWS FROM LONG-TERM FUNDS (percent)

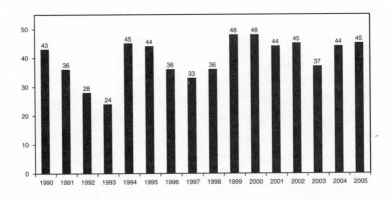

SOURCE: ICI, "Competition in the Mutual Fund Business," *Research Commentary*, January 2006, http://www.ici.org/pdf/rc_competition.pdf (accessed February 16, 2007), 2.

It is thus something of a paradox that an industry that exhibits such a competitive structure, and that offers its services to customers who are clearly willing and able in large numbers to move their business from one fund to another, should also exhibit the wide dispersion in pricing described in chapter 1. We believe the explanation for this, as described in detail in the next chapter, is the way the fund industry is regulated, and in particular what is in effect rate regulation by fund boards of directors.

The Change in Fund Distribution

The mutual fund business comprises a number of different functions, including investment management, trading, and distribution. For many years after the start of the industry, the investment advisory companies that created mutual funds usually also handled their distribution or underwriting. For funds created by securities companies, it was natural to integrate underwriting with fund management, since underwriting securities was already a core specialty of those firms.

In the last two decades, however, this vertical structure has changed dramatically. For one thing, many investors now rely on an independent financial adviser to manage their assets. The ICI now estimates that, of shareholders who own mutual funds outside of defined-contribution plans, over 80 percent have purchased funds through brokers or other advisers, with almost 50 percent going solely through professional financial advisers and 33 percent through financial advisers and other sources. Only 14 percent of these shareholders did not buy any of their shares through the intervention of a financial adviser.[13] The adviser may be a securities broker or a financial planner or carry some other title, but in all cases the distinguishing feature is that the adviser purports to be offering neutral advice to the investor. This requires a willingness to recommend funds from different fund families, and not necessarily a family with which the adviser is affiliated. For securities firms that have mutual fund arms, this has created some awkwardness; their brokers were reluctant, despite somewhat better commissions for selling in-house brands, to give preference to funds belonging to the firm's proprietary fund family unless their track record was as good as those of independently managed funds. This induced securities firms, in competing for customers, to develop an "open platform," offering funds from multiple fund families in order to capture the business of investors searching for the best investment products.

Their success in marketing these open platforms, purportedly offering the "best of breed" fund options for investors, has apparently persuaded some securities firms that they should simply go into the fund platform landlord business itself rather than offer their own funds. Thus in recent years Merrill Lynch sold its investment management business to Blackrock Financial, American Express spun out its investment management function to Ameriprise Financial, and Citigroup exchanged its asset management business for Legg Mason's brokerage network. The last transaction is particularly ironic, because banking organizations at one time envied the ability of the securities industry to offer mutual funds to its customers and fought for a relaxation of the Glass-Steagall Act and other restrictions on bank securities activities. Now it appears, only twenty years after banks were finally permitted to offer mutual funds to their customers, that they are finding the business not as attractive as they originally thought.

Thus the mutual fund industry has been evolving away from its original home in the securities industry—first as a source of underwriting and brokerage fees, and then as an advisory product—toward offering a specialized service sold to customers by unrelated third parties. By 2006 nearly 60 percent of fund sponsors were independent investment advisers, 7 percent were brokerage firms, 11 percent were banks or thrifts, and 10 percent were insurance companies.[14]

Correspondingly, the compensation of these intermediaries has changed. As investors increasingly consult brokers and financial advisers about what funds to buy, mutual fund groups have moved away from front-end loads toward continuing compensation arrangements for intermediaries through 12b-1 fees, which the SEC approved in 1980. Recipients of these fees include retirement plan recordkeepers and discount brokers as well as traditional financial advisers. The fees pay for initial sales (40 percent) and ongoing shareholder services (52 percent), as well as payment to underwriters (6 percent). The balance (2 percent) is used for promotion and advertising.[15]

The changes in fund distribution patterns have added to the competitive stress on the industry, since it is no longer in control of its distribution channels. Fund families are competing with one another not only at the point of sale, but also to attract the interest of distributors who will bring their products to that point.

The Developing Competition for Collectively Managed Assets

Even as the competitive environment within the mutual fund industry has become more challenging, new competitors outside the industry have begun to appear. These competitors are still small in relation to the giant mutual fund industry, but some are growing fast. Mutual funds will have to be nimble and efficient to hold their own, and changes in their regulatory structure will be necessary, in our view, to enable them to meet this challenge.

Separately Managed Accounts (SMAs). The move toward open platform mutual fund distribution by securities firms has been accompanied by the development of a new asset diversification vehicle that now competes with the mutual fund model. As securities firms began opening their platforms to other, "best of breed" mutual funds, some apparently realized that there was a market in offering customized advisory services themselves—not through traditional fund management, but instead by creating the equivalent of special diversified accounts customized for their brokerage clients. Hence was born the "separately managed account," or SMA, in the early 1990s. Actually, SMAs have never been completely customized, but rather are based on a common pattern and perhaps tailored or tweaked a bit in each case to suit the investment tastes and objectives of individual clients. Because this customization is somewhat labor intensive, brokerage firms limit the SMA to their wealthier clients, typically those with at least $100,000 to invest, and then charge management fees of up to 2.25 percent of assets to manage the client's portfolio—with higher-end investors typically able to negotiate lower fees.[16]

SMAs not only are customized but have other advantages for their investors as well, although the fees investors end up paying can often exceed those they would pay for a mutual fund of a similar style. Brokerage firms seem to be able to charge the extra fees for the extra services, which include more transparency about the composition of the asset portfolio, the ability for the investor to fund the account not only with cash but also with other securities he or she already may have in the brokerage account, and the simplified nature of the fee (typically a single charge, calculated as a percentage of assets and levied annually). Perhaps most important, since the assets are held in the client's name, the client can decide when to realize capital gains or losses on individual stocks rather than have to delegate that important function to the investment manager of a mutual fund and possibly suffer adverse tax consequences.

Since they were first offered, SMAs have grown substantially in asset volume, from $185 billion in 1996 to $806 billion in the third quarter of 2006 (figure 3-7). The number of these accounts also has grown, although not as rapidly as assets, from 1.66 million in 2001 to an estimated 2.52 million in the third quarter of 2006.[17] By 2006 the average account size was $295,000, well above the typical account minimum of $100,000.[18]

FIGURE 3-7
NET ASSETS OF U.S. SEPARATELY MANAGED ACCOUNTS
(Billions of dollars)

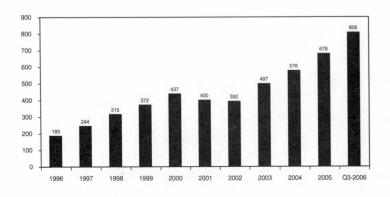

SOURCE: Financial Research Corporation, unpublished data.

Bank Common Trust Funds. Long before securities firms got into the individual money management business, bank trust departments had been managing money for their wealthy trust fund clients. Although these trusts typically have been less flexible than mutual funds and have catered to a different type of client, they have competed to some degree with their more flexible mutual fund counterparts.

As of year-end 2004, the last year for which data have been reported, the American Bankers Association reported data for only 116 bank trust departments, but these banks collectively managed $780 billion in assets (a figure that at that time exceeded the total assets of SMAs managed by securities firms).[19] These funds are held as common or commingled trust funds in which individual clients have an account.

Bank common trust funds differ from mutual funds in some important ways. First, whereas mutual fund investors can redeem their shares at virtually any time at their NAV, trust beneficiaries are subject to the terms of the trust, which may make the assets illiquid. Second, although mutual fund shareholders may select the investment strategy for their portfolios, banks make most of the investment decisions on the beneficiaries' behalf. As to corporate governance, the bank is the corporate trustee of the common trust fund; there is no other governing body. The bank itself is responsible for making all decisions, but it may outsource management tasks. Because the individuals participating in a common trust fund are already paying a trustee's fee to the bank, there is usually no separate fee paid for management of the collective investment.

In 1996 Congress gave banks authority to convert their common trust funds to a mutual fund structure. Several banks immediately took advantage of this option, including First Union (now Wachovia), Mercantile Bankshares of Baltimore, and First Chicago Bank. However, as Citigroup's sale of its mutual fund business indicates, the evolution of the market toward management by specialized advisory groups may mean that these banks will eventually abandon the advisory business in favor of offering their customers access to mutual funds managed by others.

Exchange-Traded Funds (ETFs). The asset diversification vehicle that perhaps competes most directly with existing mutual funds is the "securitized" version of a mutual fund, the exchange-traded fund, or ETF. Shares in an ETF originate when the "creation unit holder" or "market-maker," frequently an institutional investor, delivers to the ETF a specified basket of securities, typically worth at least $1 million, whose composition resembles that of the fund's existing portfolio. In exchange for this basket, the ETF issues to the market-maker a large block of shares—50,000, for example—known as a "creation unit." The market-maker then divides the creation unit and sells individual shares to the public through a secondary market such as a stock exchange. Unlike mutual fund owners, ETF investors do not buy shares at their NAV; rather, they purchase them on an exchange at the price set by the market.

The first ETF was developed in Canada and began selling in 1989 on the Toronto Stock Exchange. Four years later the first ETF was traded in the United States, on the American Stock Exchange. Up to now, all ETFs have been passively managed (like index funds) and, like traditional investment companies, can operate as either closed- or open-end funds. A closed-end ETF, or unit investment trust (UIT), raises capital primarily through an initial public offering (IPO), and once it raises enough capital, the ETF ceases to issue new shares. Open-end ETFs, on the other hand, accept additional baskets of securities, which in turn generate new shares for investors. All ETFs of both types created to date attempt to track either a broad market index,

FIGURE 3-8

NET ASSETS OF U.S. EXCHANGE-TRADED FUNDS BY LEGAL STRUCTURE

(Billions of dollars)

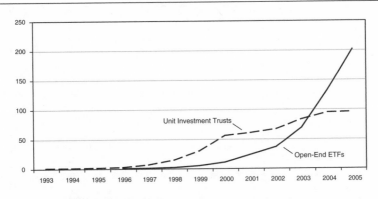

SOURCE: ICI, *2006 Investment Company Fact Book*, 27.

such as the S&P 500, the NASDAQ 100, or the Russell 2000, or an industry-specific index. The first U.S. ETF tracked the S&P 500, and its shares were given the name Standard & Poor's Depository Receipts (SPDRs, often called "SPiDeRs").

ETFs have grown rapidly in the U.S. capital markets since they were first introduced. As figure 3-8 shows, their total net assets rose from less than $1 billion in 1993 to almost $300 billion by December 2005, split roughly one-third in UITs and two-thirds in open-ended funds. Correspondingly, as figure 3-9 reveals, the total number of ETFs in the United States has increased from just 1 in 1993 to approximately 350 by December 2006.[20]

The future appears bright for ETFs: in a survey of 2,500 investment advisers, 72 percent indicated that they expected to increase their use of ETFs, 28 percent planned to keep their usage the same, and none said they would be scaling back. One expert has projected that ETF assets will reach almost $900 billion by 2010.[21] The SEC is now working on a regulation that would permit ETFs to begin operating without specific, case-by-case approval by the Commission. (SEC approval has been required in each case up to now because the ETF form requires exemptions from a large number of ICA provisions and SEC regulations.) If this regulation is ultimately

FIGURE 3-9
NUMBER OF U.S. EXCHANGE-TRADED FUNDS

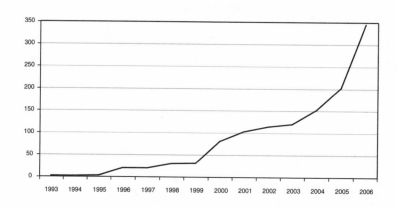

SOURCE: ICI, *2006 Investment Company Fact Book*, 28 and "Exchange-Traded Fund Assets, December 2006," http://www.ici.org/stats/latest/etfs_12_06.html (accessed February 16, 2007).

adopted, it will substantially reduce the cost of starting a new ETF and the speed with which it can be brought to market. Both reforms will certainly increase the number and competitive impact of ETFs.

ETFs have several advantages relative to mutual funds, which help account for their popularity. For one thing, they are cheaper to operate since they do not need to manage investor relationships or even keep track of them. Second, open-end ETFs do not penalize existing shareholders when additional investors buy ETF shares. When investors buy into a conventional mutual fund, the transaction costs incurred in buying new securities are spread among all existing fund shareholders. In contrast, the buyer of an ETF share pays only the incremental transactions costs he or she imposes on the market-maker. Third, since ETFs are traded on a stock exchange, their shares are priced continuously throughout the day, rather than once at the end of each day as with mutual fund shares. This makes ETFs more flexible instruments for short-term traders while avoiding the risk of market timing that has plagued some mutual funds in recent years. As described in chapter 2, the ability to "market time" arises mainly because of the lapse in time between when investors purchase a mutual fund share and when it is actually priced.

Finally, ETFs are advantageous for longer-term investors as well, since they are more tax efficient. With mutual funds, investors are at the mercy of purchase and sale decisions made by the investment manager, who can trigger capital gains by selling stocks with a low cost basis, regardless of the tax consequences for the individual shareholder. In contrast, since ETF shares are like shares of stock, the purchaser's basis is their value on the date of purchase, and no gain or loss is realized until the ETF shares are sold. Also, institutional investors and retail investors with at least 50,000 shares can redeem their shares—or whole creation units—for the underlying securities in place of cash, allowing them to manage their gains and losses still more efficiently.

However, there are also drawbacks to ETFs relative to mutual funds, and, depending on the investor, some are likely to be decisive. First, although an ETF's expenses are lower than those of the typical mutual fund, investors who purchase ETF shares pay brokerage fees, as they would with a stock. Many mutual funds, in contrast, are no-load and therefore carry no initial purchase fee, and no redemption fee provided the investor has held the shares for a sufficiently long period. Second, investors can purchase mutual fund shares in any dollar amount (usually above some minimum). ETF purchasers, on the other hand, if they want to minimize brokerage costs, must buy their shares in round lots of 100 shares. This makes it less convenient for many smaller investors to purchase ETF shares.

At this writing the SEC was considering at least one proposal to create an actively managed ETF.[22] Because of the various advantages of the ETF structure just noted, actively managed ETFs might have significant advantages over actively managed mutual funds for some investors. In order to grant its approval, however, the SEC must sort through some difficult issues, such as how often an actively managed ETF must disclose the composition of its portfolio, and exactly what basket of securities an investor in such an ETF would be purchasing, given that both the ETF itself and the contents of the ETF's portfolio would be traded throughout the day.

Mutual funds may face an even stiffer challenge from ETFs if the sponsors of these instruments figure out ways to accommodate the desire of individual investors to invest fixed dollar sums on a regular basis, rather than accumulate enough cash to buy round lots. Already ETFs are being marketed to companies as investment vehicles for retirement accounts, and companies can aggregate the orders of their many employees to allow for small contributions out of each paycheck. If ETF sponsors can figure out ways to aggregate such small contributions on their own, they will pose an even more direct competitive challenge to mutual funds in the future.

Hedge Funds. In recent years, hedge funds—collective investment vehicles exempt from registration under the ICA—have been the most rapidly growing structure for collective investment. Although a relatively young investment vehicle, hedge funds had attracted well above $1 trillion globally by mid-2006. Because the funds are not registered with the SEC, no official data on their number or size exist. Figure 3-10 illustrates the rapid growth in hedge funds as estimated by one industry source.

FIGURE 3-10
ESTIMATED ASSETS OF HEDGE FUNDS WORLDWIDE
(Billions of dollars)

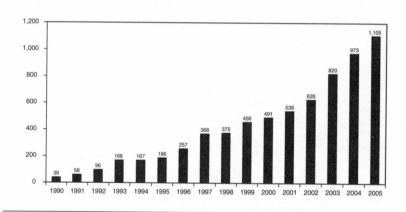

SOURCE: Hedge Fund Research, Inc., *Hedge Fund Industry Report, Year-End 2005.*

In a broad sense, mutual funds and hedge funds are similar in that both afford investors the ability to invest in a pool of diversified assets. But the easy comparison essentially stops there. For one thing, to avoid having to register with the SEC, hedge funds rely on two "private" investment company exclusions in sections 3(c)(1) and 3(c)(7) of the ICA. Section 3(c)(1) requires the fund to have less than one hundred investors and forbids the fund from making a public offering of its securities. Also, under the SEC's Regulation D, hedge funds are limited to offering their securities to "accredited" investors, those with substantial annual incomes (above $200,000 for individuals, $300,000 for families) and assets (individual or joint net worth with one's spouse exceeding $1 million, or corporations or other institutional entities with assets above $5 million). The SEC has recently proposed increasing the minimum net worth for an individual accredited investor to $2.5 million.[23] A fund that operates under section 3(c)(7) may sell its securities only to "qualified purchasers," which can be a person who owns not less than $5 million in investments, a family-owned company with not less than $5 million in investments, certain trusts, or another entity such as an institutional investor that owns not less than $25 million in investments. In addition, although the ICA does not limit the number of investors of 3(c)(7) funds, the funds themselves limit investors to 499 in order to avoid public reporting requirements under the 1934 Act.[24]

Mutual funds, on the other hand, have no such income or wealth restrictions. Because hedge funds are not registered with the SEC or regulated by any other government agency, they can borrow to increase their leverage, and they can engage in a variety of investment activities—notably short selling, currency arbitrage, and taking interests in credit default swaps, options, and other derivatives—that are off limits to mutual funds. (Mutual funds may engage in some of those activities if they are "covered," which as a practical matter makes them financially unattractive.) In addition, hedge funds are not restricted in the formulas they may use to compensate their management.

The continued growth and lack of transparency (some would say mystery) surrounding hedge funds have led to calls for their regulation. In 2004 the SEC proposed a rule that would have required the registration of hedge fund managers, but the rule was struck down by the Court of Appeals for the D.C. Circuit. However, the debate over the wisdom of regulating versus simply monitoring hedge funds is not of central interest here. The relevant point is that because they are unregulated and have greater freedom of activity, hedge funds have been an increasingly popular alternative to mutual funds as investments for people of means. In addition, there is anecdotal evidence that their substantially higher compensation structure and lack of regulatory "hassle" are luring management talent away from the mutual fund industry. As a result, hedge funds exert significant competitive pressure on the mutual fund industry.

Conclusion

In sum, although the mutual fund industry has been fabulously successful in attracting the interest of American investors, it now faces a future in which it will have to fight for continued growth with competitors such as SMAs, ETFs, and hedge funds, all of which offer advantages that heavily regulated mutual funds cannot easily match. Over the past decade, these alternative collective investment vehicles have experienced solid rates of annual growth in assets, typically surpassing that of the mutual fund industry. Although such impressive growth rates—especially for ETFs—are partly attributable to their more recent emergence, industry commentators expect this robust growth to continue.[25]

Consequently, it appears that the best path for the mutual fund industry is to emphasize its potential as the lowest-cost provider of collective investment services for the vast American middle class. However, as the discussion thus far has suggested, and as discussed in detail in the succeeding chapters, the mutual fund industry has not yet demonstrated an ability to reduce its costs as far as it might. Despite huge numbers of competing funds and fund managers, price competition is weak, and mutual funds are likely to be operating very inefficiently. Accordingly, the task for the industry and for policymakers is to break down the structures—regulatory or otherwise—that are preventing an industry with so many competitors, within and without, from reaching its full potential.

4

The Paradox of Mutual Fund Fees

We all want to pay less for what we buy, and mutual fund investors presumably are no exception. The advantage of competitive markets—those with plenty of competitors and potential entrants—is that competition ensures that prices are as close as possible to marginal cost, or the cost of producing one additional unit of a product or service. If prices in such a market rise above marginal cost for any sustained period, existing firms will reap juicy profits, inducing other companies to enter the market, forcing prices back down and competing those extra profits away. Conversely, if prices fall below marginal cost for too long, existing firms either will cut back on production or quality or leave entirely.

In the last chapter we demonstrated that, by the measures most used by economists and government authorities to assess the strength of competition, the mutual fund industry is highly competitive. If that were not enough, the industry has a collection of competing products nipping at its heels.

It is thus with some irony, and frankly some puzzlement on our part as we started this study, that the mutual fund industry has been the subject of attack on the one dimension of its activity where one would assume that competition would be working best—its fees, or more accurately, the fees charged by its investment advisers. For example, one of the industry's iconic figures, John Bogle, who vaulted the Vanguard fund family to a leading position in the industry, has lambasted fund managers for imposing "excessive costs," and fund boards for allowing that to occur.[1] He is hardly the only critic. David Swensen, the highly regarded investment manager for Yale University, has leveled a similar set of criticisms, charging that investors pay high fees for mediocre performance. The root of the problem, he argues, seconding Bogle, is the failure of fund directors to police the fees and expenses of investment advisers.[2]

Indeed, complaints about mutual fund fees antedate the recent critiques by Bogle and Swensen. In 2000, as noted in chapter 1, the Government Accountability Office concluded after an extensive study that "the structure and nature of competition in the mutual fund industry appear to resemble the type of market referred to by economists as 'monopolistic competition.'" The GAO went on to explain: "Industries where monopolistic competition prevails usually have large numbers of firms and easy industry entry, but products are differentiated by characteristics, such as quality or service. Because their products differ, firms can charge different prices from other firms in the industry. This ability to distinguish one firm's product from that of others, results in somewhat higher pricing levels than would result from a perfectly competitive market."[3] In other words, markets with monopolistically competitive pricing can exhibit wide price dispersion because small differences in products or services among firms in the market reduce direct competition.

However, as we showed in chapter 1 and will demonstrate in more detail below, very substantial disparities prevail in mutual fund pricing despite a lack of any obvious differences in products or services. Accordingly, in a widely noted paper published in 2001, two scholars, John Freeman and Stewart Brown, pointed out that "SEC regulation [of the mutual fund industry] can be detailed and complex, but it has not generated any semblance of intra-industry competition on the part of equity fund advisors."[4]

This view is not universally shared. As noted in chapter 1, two well-known scholars, John Coates and Glenn Hubbard, cited very much the same evidence we highlighted in the last chapter about the structure of the mutual fund industry to argue that the industry is in fact competitive.[5] Seventeen years ago a team of Princeton economists and an independent economic consultant reached a similar conclusion.[6] Under these conditions, critiques of "excessive costs" should not be credible.

In this chapter we attempt to sort out this seeming paradox: why a competitive industry, with virtually identical products, continues to receive serious criticism about excessive prices. Generations of economists would insist that such a thing is not possible, but there it is. We reach a result similar to that of the critics, but we come to a far different conclusion about the causes and remedies.

The Variation in Expense Ratios

Pricing in the mutual fund market can be difficult to describe or categorize, much less explain or justify. Ultimately, however, the price for a fund adviser's service in providing collective investment management is the sum of the fees and expenses it charges (not counting any "load," which is a sales charge), usually stated as a percentage of assets, and called its "expense ratio." Thus the terms "fees and expenses," "prices," and "costs"—usually expressed as the expense ratio—have been and will be used interchangeably in this book. It is the disparity in these prices that lends support to the GAO's view that the mutual fund market exhibits monopolistic competition.

The data on index fund pricing are especially interesting. The management of an index fund involves virtually no research, analysis, or stock picking, since the fund attempts simply to replicate a particular index of share prices, such as the S&P 500.[7] The only role for a manager of such a fund is to maintain the comparability between the shares in the fund and the shares in the chosen index. Table 4-1 lists most of the funds with assets over $200 million that seek to match the S&P 500 and reports their expense ratios. (Vanguard funds have been excluded for reasons discussed later in this chapter.) To focus on the management costs included in fund pricing, table 4-1 shows the expense ratios net of any 12b-1 fees, although where 12b-1 fees are charged, that fact is noted in the table.

The table is instructive for a number of reasons. Despite the fact that the actual services of these funds are roughly the same, and their performance cannot be considered a significant factor in investor choice, the expense ratios vary widely. In addition, and most important for our analysis, the management fees of the listed funds vary quite significantly, although all are engaged in exactly the same task: tracking the S&P 500 index. The management fees range from a low of 5 basis points in the small DWS fund to a high of 25 basis points for the relatively large Dreyfus fund, all for basically the same function and, of course, virtually identical performance. Hence the question: If these mutual funds are competitive but offering the same service, why aren't they charging roughly the same price?

This variation in fees also shows up in other fund categories. A sample of various kinds of funds, reported by the mutual fund research firm Morningstar, shows a range of costs, excluding 12b-1 fees (table 4-2). In

TABLE 4-1

FEES, EXPENSE RATIOS, AND ASSETS OF S&P 500 INDEX FUNDS

(Percent except where stated otherwise)

Fund and Ticker Symbol	Front-End Load	Management Fee	12b-1 Fee	Expense Ratio Net of 12b-1 Fee	Assests (Billions of Dollars)
Schwab S&P 500 Index Investor (SWPIX)	0.00	0.09	0.00	0.37	8.1
T. Rowe Price Equity Index 500 (PREIX)	0.00	0.15	0.00	0.35	7.5
Dreyfus S&P 500 Index (PEOPX)	0.00	0.25	0.00	0.50	3.7
Gartmore S&P 500 Index A (GRMAX)	5.75	0.13	0.25	0.25	3.5
MainStay S&P 500 Index A (MSXAX)	3.00	0.24	0.25	0.48	1.7
Morgan Stanley S&P 500 Index A (SPIAX)	5.25	0.12	0.24	0.38	1.2
Principal Inv Large Cap S&P 500 Index A (PLSAX)	1.50	0.15	0.15	0.49	1.0
Munder Index 500 A (MUXAX)	2.50	0.12	0.25	0.41	0.9
DWS S&P 500 Index A (SXPAX)	4.50	0.05	0.25	0.41	0.7
State Farm S&P 500 Index A Legacy (SLIAX)	5.00	0.20	0.25	0.55	0.6
Legg Mason Partners S&P 500 Index A (SBSPX)	0.00	0.25	0.20	0.39	0.5
United Association S&P 500 Index II (UAIIX)	0.00	0.10	0.05	0.12	0.4
AIM S&P 500 Index Inv (ISPIX)	0.00	0.25	0.25	0.60	0.2
UBS S&P 500 Index A (PSPIX)	2.50	0.20	0.25	0.70	0.2

SOURCE: Morningstar, www.morningstar.com (accessed December 22, 2006).
NOTE: Data are as of December 22, 2006. All funds have a minimum initial investment of $2,500 or less. Certain funds were removed because their expense ratios provided by Morningstar were temporarily discounted.

TABLE 4-2

EXPENSE-RATIO RANGES FOR VARIOUS MUTUAL FUND CATEGORIES

| | Lower-End Expense Ratio | | Higher-End Expense Ratio | | |
| | Expense | | Including | Net of | |
Fund Style	Ratio	Fund Name	12b-1 Fee	12b-1 Fee	Fund Name
Large-Cap Value	0.52	Dodge & Cox Stock (DODGX)	2.65	1.65	Saratoga Large Capitalization Value B (SLVZX)
Large-Cap Blend	0.57	Fidelity Fund (FFIDX)	2.43	1.68	Dreyfus Premier Growth & Income B (PEGBX)
Large-Cap Growth	0.66[a]	American Funds Growth Fund of America A (AGTHX)	3.29	3.23	Reynolds Fund (REYFX)
Mid-Cap Value	0.82	T. Rowe Price Mid-Cap Value (TRMCX)	2.41	1.41	Quaker Mid-Cap Value C (QMCCX)
Mid-Cap Blend	0.89	FPA Paramount (FPRAX)	2.59	1.59	Calvert Mid Cap Value C (CMVCX)
Mid-Cap Growth	0.72	Fidelity Mid-Cap Stock (FMCSX)	2.65	2.15	Integrity Small Cap Growth A (ICPAX)
Small-Cap Value	1.00	Northern Small Cap Value (NOSGX)	2.60	2.60	Dean Small Cap Value C (DACCX)
Small-Cap Blend	0.84	T. Rowe Price Small-Cap Value (PRSVX)	2.69	1.69	Quaker Small-Cap Value B (QSVBX)
Small-Cap Growth	0.87	Janus Venture (JAVTX)	4.24	3.24	Jundt U.S. Emerging Growth B (JEGBX)

SOURCE: Morningstar, www.morningstar.com (accessed July 26, 2006).
NOTE: Data are as of July 26, 2006.
a. Includes 12b-1 fee of 0.25 percent.

preparing the table, we eliminated the two funds in each category that had the highest and lowest total fees, to provide a sense of the range even when outliers are excluded. Also, the Vanguard funds have again been excluded, for reasons that will be discussed later.

Aside from the difficulty in explaining the variation in fees across funds in the same or similar investment categories for seemingly identical services, this variation also presents potential investors with several decisions that can be difficult to evaluate. How does an investor decide, for example, whether 20 or 25 basis points is reasonable for a 12b-1 fee? Why pay such a fee at all

TABLE 4-3

RETURNS OF SELECTED MUTUAL FUNDS WITH HIGH AND LOW EXPENSES

Fund and Ticker Symbol	Sales Load		Expense Ratio	12b-1 Fee	Manage-ment Fee	Total Return (percent a year)			
	Front-End	Back-End				1 yr	3 yr	5 yr	10yr
Fidelity Mid-Cap Stock (FMCSX)	0.00	0.00	0.72	0.00	0.45	10.62	14.28	3.78	12.81
Phoenix Mid-Cap Growth A (PHSKX)	5.75	0.00	1.53	0.25	0.83	-4.08	6.45	0.15	4.72
Vanguard Equity-Income (VEIPX)	0.00	0.00	0.31	0.00	0.30	7.23	12.85	5.61	9.57
First American Large Cap Value B (FATBX)	0.00	5.00	1.92	1.00	0.65	6.29	11.80	3.03	6.24

SOURCE: Morningstar, www.morningstar.com (accessed July 21, 2006).
NOTE: Data are as of July 21, 2006. Both the Fidelity and Phoenix funds and the Vanguard and First American funds are in the same Morningstar categories, mid-cap growth and large-cap value respectively.

when other funds don't even charge it? What additional services does, say, the Reynolds Fund provide that make it worth paying an expense ratio almost five times that of the American Funds equivalent in the same (large-cap growth) category?

One might suppose that fund performance must account for such price disparities, but that does not seem to be a factor. For example, as table 4-3 shows, the Phoenix Mid-Cap Growth A fund, with total expenses of 153 basis points, was twice as expensive—even before the 5.75 percent load— as the Fidelity Mid-Cap Stock fund, which has no front-end load and total expenses of 72 basis points. Yet the Phoenix fund's performance over the last one, three, five, and ten years is actually weaker than that of its Fidelity counterpart. Nor are these results unique—they can be duplicated in any cursory review of the relevant Morningstar data, and they are of course consistent with the efficient market hypothesis, which holds that even professional investors cannot beat the market over the long term. Hot hands may produce superior performance over the short term, but over long periods the results of all funds tend to regress to the mean.

To see that the dispersion in prices extends beyond the few funds listed in the tables, turn back to figure 1-1 in chapter 1, which shows the wide dispersion of costs for the class A shares of 811 actively managed U.S. equity funds. (As chapter 1 noted, this figure omits the 3 percent of funds at both extremes and deducts 25 basis points for comparability across funds with and without 12b-1 fees, to come up with a total of 811 funds.) The figure shows a distribution of expense ratios of about 300 percent; that is, the most expensive funds are about three times as costly as the least expensive ones.

Any reader who imagines that, for some unknown reason, the collective investment world has to be one of widely differing prices should also look again at figure 1-2, which shows the dispersion of fund expense ratios (again eliminating outliers) for 456 equity funds sold in the United Kingdom. This cost distribution is considerably tighter than that in the United States: the highest-cost fund is only about 50 percent more costly than the lowest-cost fund. (It is slightly higher if one subtracts 25 basis points from each expense ratio to account for possible inclusion of the equivalent of a 12b-1 fee.)

U.S. and U.K. equity funds differ in another important way. According to a report by Lipper, another mutual fund research company, the dispersion of U.K. funds *on a weighted-average basis* is also much narrower than that among U.S. funds. A weighted-average basis gives more mathematical weight to larger funds when striking an average, since the size of a fund tends to correlate with the number of accounts. Figure 4-1 (on the following page), taken from that Lipper report, shows the disparity between the lowest and highest expense ratios among funds in the United States, and the United Kingdom, on a weighted-average basis. The near absence of any difference among U.K. funds suggests intense competition for investors among U.K. advisers.[8]

This phenomenon of price convergence also occurs in the U.S. market for separately managed accounts. In the SMA industry, a registered representative at a firm such as Ameriprise or Smith Barney serves as an intermediary between the investor and a money management firm. Money managers devise basic personal account strategies—for example, accounts concentrated in small-cap stocks—and market them to registered representatives at retail brokerage firms, typically offering fee breakpoints for larger accounts. Depending on the brokerage firm, either the registered representatives

FIGURE 4-1

ASSET-WEIGHTED EXPENSE RATIOS OF U.S. AND U.K. MUTUAL FUNDS

(Percent of assets)

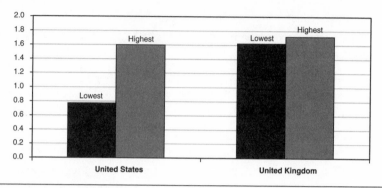

SOURCE: Lipper, "A Comparison of Mutual Fund Expenses Across the Atlantic," Lipper Fund*Industry* Insight Reports, September 2005.

themselves, the research staff of the firm, or the overlay manager (an outside firm contracted by the brokerage firm) will choose from among these accounts and then use them to set up SMAs for individual clients, modifying them according to the clients' specific preferences, either customizing the holdings or implementing tax-efficiency measures. Furthermore, depending on the size, capabilities, and administrative arrangements of the brokerage firm, the adviser, the money manager, the overlay manager, or the brokerage firm itself may execute the trades for the SMA customer. It is noteworthy that the money management firms that offer these personal account strategies do not have to get the approval of a board of directors in order to establish their pricing.[9] Figure 4-2 depicts the "list-price" fees of 1,462 basic account strategies offered by money management firms, from which registered representatives choose in order to create SMAs for their individual clients. Because the money management firms set their own prices and compete to attract the business of registered representatives, one would expect to see much less price dispersion than for mutual fund expense ratios. And this is precisely what the data show. Of the fees for the 1,462 accounts, 65 percent fall between 0.75 and 1.0 percent and 85 percent between 0.50 and 1.00 percent of assets.

FIGURE 4-2

DISTRIBUTION OF FEES CHARGED BY MONEY MANAGEMENT
FIRMS FOR BASIC ACCOUNT STRATEGIES USED IN SMAs
(1,462 Strategies)

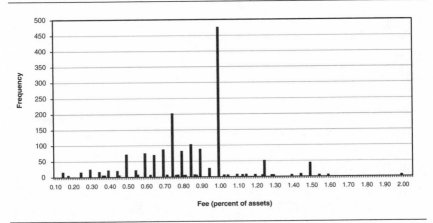

SOURCE: Morningstar, *Morningstar Principia Separate Accounts*, December 2006. To exclude outliers, we removed the top and bottom 3 percent of the basic account strategies from the original sample, as we did with the U.S. and U.K. mutual fund samples.

Finally, it is sometimes argued that competition is stronger, and the dispersion of expense ratios much narrower, among the largest U.S. funds than across the whole fund universe. That is true, but only to a limited extent, and only if we continue to exclude Vanguard funds. Table 1-1 showed that the dispersion of expense ratios for comparable funds of the ten largest and most competitive U.S. mutual fund families is still considerably wider than the dispersion among our sample of *all* U.K. equity funds. Among these ten families (again if we ignore Vanguard, which in all cases would widen the dispersion to 300 percent), the highest expense ratio exceeds the lowest by between 100 percent and somewhat more than 200 percent, depending on the fund category.

What could account for these disparities? More important, how can such disparities persist in an industry that exhibits all the other characteristics of competition? These are important questions, because disparities like these are a sign that mutual fund investors are not getting the benefit of vigorous price competition in an industry that by all accounts should be competitive.[10] In the rest of this chapter we first consider and reject some possible answers offered by others and then present our own.

Conventional Explanations of Expense Ratio Variations

Two broad explanations are conventionally offered for why mutual fund prices differ so much from one another. One is that the funds themselves are organizationally flawed. Their governance structure, it is alleged, leads to failure of oversight of fund managers. The other is that fees are so bewildering and disclosure so poor that confused investors cannot figure out how to differentiate between expensive and inexpensive funds.

Industry Structure. Of the two explanations, the organizational argument is the more interesting, at least to us, because mutual funds are indeed uniquely organized. As we discussed in detail in chapters 1 and 2, funds are generally established by an investment advisory firm, which undertakes the initial capital investment to create a fund, register it with the SEC, and appoint the first board of directors, a majority of which will, under current SEC rules, likely be independent of the adviser. Each fund is a separate corporation with its own board of directors, although the same board may oversee many individual funds—perhaps 100 or more—within the same fund group. The fund in turn contracts with the investment adviser to furnish not only investment advice but all other management functions. Funds typically have no staff of their own.

This structure, critics argue, creates a conflict of interest between the investment adviser and the fund's shareholders in that the adviser wants to earn as much as possible from the relationship with the fund, whereas the shareholders want the adviser's services at the lowest possible cost. The SEC has accepted this view, noting in a 1992 report that "fees paid from an investment company's assets to sponsors [usually the investment adviser] and their affiliates—whether advisers' fees, principal underwriting fees, distribution fees, or fees for other services—directly affect shareholders' investment return. The higher the fee, the lower the return. The conflict of interest is inherent."[11]

Similarly, some observers of the mutual fund industry lament that funds are captives of their advisers, and that even though boards of directors have the authority to terminate an advisory contract, they almost never do, and thus are not truly free to ask a number of advisers to bid for the opportunity to advise the fund. This idea seems to have originated with the SEC's

1966 report to Congress. There the Commission noted, "The unaffiliated directors are not in a position to bargain on an equal footing with the adviser on matters of such crucial importance to it. They are not free, as a practical matter, to terminate established management relationships when differences arise over the advisory fees or other compensation. . . . For these reasons, arm's-length bargaining between the unaffiliated directors and the managers on these matters is a wholly unrealistic alternative."[12]

This 1966 report and its views on the relationship between advisers and the funds they manage formed the basis for the ICA amendments of 1970. These included section 36(b), which embedded in the law a view of the mutual fund industry that has had important and—as we will argue—harmful effects on competition.

The focus on the relationship between the adviser and the fund, although seductive, is largely illusory. Among other things, it is the wrong issue. If the mutual fund industry were characterized by vigorous price competition, it would not matter how the fees and expenses charged to funds by their advisers are determined; advisers would not be able to charge substantially more than the market price for equivalent service. Unless the advisers themselves face competition from other advisers—the kind of competition that forces sellers to find more efficient ways of operating—the prices they offer to the funds they manage will never reflect the low costs to investors that competition could produce. The real issue, then, is not how to structure the relationship between adviser and fund, but why it is that the industry does not exhibit vigorous price competition.

Because the SEC has apparently accepted the conventional analysis that high fees and expenses result from the weak bargaining position of the independent directors, its policy over the years has been to increase the percentage of independent directors on fund boards. As noted in chapter 2, the ICA itself requires only that 40 percent of a fund's directors be "disinterested" (that is, independent), but the SEC has conditioned eligibility for many important exemptions from the ICA on funds having a board made up of a majority of independent directors, and in some cases a supermajority of 75 percent. A logical extension of this policy would be to empower independent directors to open the advisory role to competitive bidding—a possibility that is no longer out of the question in the view of some members and observers of the industry.[13]

Most recently, as we discussed in chapter 2, after the late-trading and market timing scandals in 2003 the SEC required that boards have an independent chair as well as a board composed of directors more than 75 percent of whom are independent. Although this requirement was struck down by the U.S. Circuit Court of Appeals,[14] its adoption by the SEC is indicative of the staff's predilections, since an independent chair and independent directors could have done nothing to prevent actions taken solely by the adviser, without any reason to inform the directors. The scandals seem to have been used as a pretext to adopt remedies for a different problem. The SEC staff's view of the importance of director independence was expressed most forcefully in its 2000 *Report on Mutual Fund Fees and Expenses*. There the staff expressed concern about the level of fees and expenses and identified further independence and power for the independent directors as one of the most important remedies: "Of particular importance is the proposal that would, in effect, require that independent directors…comprise at least a majority of the members of fund boards. In our view, a fund board that has at least a majority of independent directors is likely to do a better job of representing the interests of fund shareholders…. An independent director majority would be able to elect officers of the fund, call meetings, solicit proxies, and take other actions without the consent of the adviser."[15]

Inadequate Disclosure. The other conventional explanation for the disparity in fees and expenses in an industry that ought to be price competitive is that investors are not well informed about these costs, or do not care about them. This argument assumes that if investors received adequate disclosure, they would be willing and able to sort out the expensive funds from the inexpensive ones, and that would introduce more price competition into the market.

Indeed, a survey done for this study by International Communications Research (ICR), a prominent survey firm, in December 2005 seems to indicate that investors are confused and unknowledgeable about the fees and expenses of the funds in which they invest. The survey confirmed that investors are not well informed and do not believe themselves to be well informed about their mutual funds.

The ICR survey showed that about half of all households own mutual funds either directly or through a retirement arrangement with their employer.

This is consistent with the industry's own estimate that roughly 90 million Americans are mutual fund investors.[16] The survey asked those respondents who were mutual fund investors to rate their knowledge of mutual funds on a scale from 1 to 10, with 10 being the highest level of knowledge and 1 the lowest. Relatively few investors considered themselves well informed about their mutual fund investments: 21 percent rated their knowledge an 8, 9, or 10, while 41 percent placed their knowledge at 1, 2, or 3.

Still fewer, even among those who thought they were well informed, actually had a strong grasp of the basic issues associated with a mutual fund investment. The issue about which investors thought they knew most was the performance of their fund investment, and the names of the fund's directors was the subject on which they claimed to know the least. However, when ICR asked those who rated their knowledge highly (8 or above) what they were actually paying as an advisory fee, only one fifth even responded with a percentage, and of these, fewer than a third cited a percentage between zero and 1.5 percent—the range in which advisory fees are usually imposed. In other words, of the one-fifth of the sample who thought they had the *highest* level of knowledge about their investments, fewer than one in ten actually knew even approximately what they were paying as an advisory fee. The remainder responded with dollar amounts, thought they were not paying advisory fees, or gave some other response.[17]

To be sure, many of these investors may hold funds through pension plans in which investments are made for them by a professional pension fund manager. Others, even those who made their investments directly, may believe that in mutual fund investing—as in virtually all other areas of the economy where competition prevails—prices are roughly the same and they need not expend time to inform themselves of these specifics. Whatever the explanation, investors *in general* do not appear concerned about mutual fund prices.

The SEC and, to its credit, the mutual fund industry have long been concerned that investors are not well informed about the expenses charged by the mutual funds they own. The SEC's solution has been to simplify disclosure by requiring, at the front of every fund prospectus, a summary statement that includes a fee table showing all the fees and expenses borne by the fund's shareholders. The SEC has also required inclusion of these items in funds' reports to shareholders.[18] Despite these and other efforts, the SEC continues to worry that shareholders are not really paying attention, noting in 2004 that "the degree to which investors understand mutual fund fees and expenses remains a source of concern."[19] In January 2004 the SEC published a proposed rule on point-of-sale disclosures, intended to further inform investors about the costs they are about to incur when they invest in a particular mutual fund.[20] For its part, the industry's trade association, the Investment Company Institute, has also been focusing on clearer and more accessible disclosure—more figures and graphs, better use of the Internet—as a way of providing investors with the information they arguably need.[21]

But do they need it? Might fees and expenses already be so low that even a threefold difference across funds does not matter to investors? The fees and expenses of a typical fund may seem small in relation to the typical fund's returns, but over time they can have a significant effect on the total return that investors receive, especially on their long-term retirement savings. John Bogle, perhaps the industry's leading critic, has shown in a number of books and articles that even small differences in fees, when cumulated over a long period, can reduce an investor's total gain substantially—by as much as 75 percent over a ten-year period.[22] One can argue with the methodology that Bogle uses,[23] but it is impossible to quarrel with the arithmetic: if fees are reduced each year by even a small percentage of a portfolio's assets, the cumulative impact over time, due to the effect of compounding yields, can be large. Bogle's solution to this problem echoes that of the SEC: more board independence.

Plausible as both ideas—greater independence for the board of directors and greater disclosure—may sound (and indeed both have resonated in parts of Congress and in the media), on closer inspection neither turns out to be satisfactory. The fundamental fact is that there is already quite a bit of director independence.[24] Most mutual funds have had a supermajority of independent directors (although not independent chairs) for many years. And the industry's disclosure obligations have already been tightened, so that now all fund prospectuses and annual reports must provide a summary statement with a box that summarizes, in dollar terms, the effect of fees on a hypothetical investment of $10,000 over one, three, five, and ten years. Yet none of this has substantially changed the industry's pricing,[25] nor has it caused investors to flee from more expensive to less expensive funds at anything like the pace one would expect in a vigorously price-competitive market. In our view, there is another answer to the puzzle, and it lies neither in the supposed lack of board independence nor in inadequate disclosure, but in the way in which mutual funds, as they are currently organized, are *regulated*.

The Fundamental Problem: The Industry's Regulatory Structure

A headline in the *Wall Street Journal* on July 5, 2006, declared, "Independent Directors Strike Back."[26] The article under the headline noted that the independent directors of the funds managed by AIM Investments were demanding that the funds lower their advisory fees. The article attributed this singular behavior to a newly installed independent chair of the mutual funds. It evidently did not seem odd to the author of the article that the independent directors of a group of mutual funds would have to demand that the adviser compete with other advisers, yet by the lights of ordinary business practice it was quite strange indeed. For some reason, the adviser to the AIM funds did not want to lower its fees and expenses in order to attract more investors. Why would it be that in the mutual fund industry, among all the industries in the United States, the principal players—the investment advisers of mutual funds—refuse to compete on price with one another?

One of the academic papers most critical of mutual fund pricing begins its analysis with this statement: "This strangeness—tremendous popularity, proliferating consumer options, and less than robust price competition—arises in the realm of the most tightly regulated financial product sold in the country today. In the words of a former SEC chairman, 'no issuer of securities is subject to more detailed regulation than a mutual fund.'"[27] But in the end, to address this "strangeness," the authors call for yet more regulation; it seems never to have occurred to them that the heavy regulation of the mutual fund industry and its peculiar price structure might be related: that regulation might be the cause of, rather than the remedy for, the industry's peculiar failure to live up to the promise of its competitive structure.

In our view the problem is not greedy advisers, co-opted boards, or inattentive or uninformed investors. The problem is regulation itself—the

fact that the ICA requires mutual funds to be structured as separate corporations, with boards of directors charged with responsibility for controlling
the adviser's fees and the fund's expenses. This unique form—an artifact of
the industry's origins in the 1920s—*makes the mutual fund industry, in effect,
a rate-regulated industry*. And as has historically been the case with rate
regulation, the result is to impair effective competition.

It is no coincidence that the unique organizational structure required of
the mutual fund industry has produced a unique system of price setting,
one that does not include vigorous price competition and the benefits that
it can bring to consumers. Price convergence—usually toward the marginal
cost of the most efficient producer—is present in most areas of the U.S.
economy, but has not occurred in the mutual fund industry. There, as
demonstrated above, fees and expenses—the price for the service of collectively managing a fund—vary widely and seemingly without relation to
service quality. The 100 percent discrepancy in expense ratios between the
Gartmore and the UBS index funds (table 4-1 above), when both offer similar services as measured by fund performance, is a case in point.

Simply put, price competition and price convergence have not occurred
in the mutual fund industry because there is little incentive for investment
advisers to reduce costs. Under section 36(b) of the ICA, the investment
advisers of mutual funds are deemed to have a "fiduciary duty with respect
to the receipt of compensation for services, or of payments of a material
nature, paid by such registered investment company... to such investment
adviser or any affiliated person of such investment adviser." The SEC, or
any investor, is specifically permitted to enforce this requirement against
the investment adviser and any other person who has a fiduciary duty with
respect to the fund, which of course includes the board of directors. Thus
every form of payment by the fund to the investment adviser—not just the
advisory fee—must not result in compensation to the adviser or its affiliates
that exceeds what the vague term "fiduciary duty" would allow, and the
members of a board of directors that approves compensation that exceeds
this permissible level are liable to suit from fund shareholders to the same
extent as the investment adviser who receives the payment.

In a series of cases testing this language, particularly *Gartenberg v.
Merrill Lynch Asset Management, Inc.*, the courts have given some content
to the term "fiduciary duty."[28] The *Gartenberg* court laid out a series of

considerations that a fund's directors must take into account when judging whether the fees and expenses charged to a fund by its adviser meet the fiduciary duty test:[29]

- the nature and quality of the adviser's services;

- the adviser's costs of providing these services;

- whether the adviser shares with the fund the economies of scale that result from growth of the fund;

- the volume of orders that the adviser must process; and

- the indirect benefits that the adviser receives as a result of operating the fund.

Note that the only objectively quantifiable elements in this list are the adviser's costs and the volume of orders. Because order processing does not involve a significant cost, and the other elements of the test are either hard to evaluate or discover, or of little significance when discovered, the directors will naturally focus on the adviser's costs. In practice, this means that fund boards of directors—when they are operating most diligently—pay considerable attention to the adviser's costs of providing a wide variety of services to the fund, with a view to determining whether these costs are within some undefined zone of reasonableness. These costs, supplemented by an allowance for profit, then become the basis for the adviser's compensation. Oddly, the *Gartenberg* court rejected comparisons with the fees and expenses of advisers to other funds as the standard to which the directors should look,[30] thus specifically precluding any director responsibility for promoting competition among funds or advisory groups.

If this focus on costs in price or rate setting sounds familiar, it is because one encounters the same focus in the rate-setting process for public utilities. One major difference is that public utilities usually have large installed fixed capital investments, whereas investment advisers tend to have large variable personnel costs. Otherwise the rate-setting process for both is similar (although, as we will shortly explain, with different types of regulators: government agencies in the case of utilities, boards of directors in the case of mutual funds) and results in similar outcomes.

Government (or for that matter any) regulation of rates or prices is subject to several well-known deficiencies, many of which are present in the mutual fund industry. As one of the country's leading regulatory economists, Alfred Kahn, wrote in his treatise, *The Economics of Regulation*, "[R]egulation as such contains no built-in mechanism for assuring efficiency. To the extent that it effectively restrains public utility companies from fully exploiting their potential monopoly power, it tends to take away any supernormal returns they might earn as a result of improvements in efficiency, thereby diminishing their incentive to try."[31]

To be sure, mutual funds are not regulated utilities and do not have monopoly power, so the quotation seems inapposite. However, it is not the funds themselves that are rate-regulated under the ICA, but the investment adviser's charges to the fund. Because there is only one adviser to the fund, *the adviser is in fact in the same position with respect to the fund as a monopoly public utility is with respect to the consumers in its market. The board of directors, then, functions in the same way that the public utility rate commission functions: it regulates or limits the profits of the adviser to be sure that consumers—the fund and, ultimately, its shareholders—are fairly treated.*

Looked at from this perspective, the analogy to public utility rate regulation actually is quite close. Let us rephrase Kahn's statement so that it applies more clearly to the mutual fund case: in controlling the degree of profit that the investment adviser earns from its services to the fund, the board weakens the incentives of the investment adviser to reduce its costs so as to earn higher profits. This appears to be what has been happening all along in the mutual fund business. The regulation of investment advisers' compensation under section 36(b) has reduced their incentive to cut costs and operate more efficiently.

There is, however, one other important respect in which the investment adviser is different from the monopoly public utility: because it has a monopoly on production in its geographic area, the public utility presumably does not have to compete with other producers in supplying, say, electricity. In contrast, competition clearly places some limit on what an adviser might charge as an advisory fee, since at some point a fee that is too high would drive investors to other funds, lowering the adviser's profit. So the question arises: would not advisers still seek to keep their fees low in order to retain investors, or—more to the point—would they not lower their fees in order to attract investors away from competing funds? If so, don't advisers still operate in a competitive market, with incentives for lower costs, innovation, and efficiency, even though they must obtain approval of their fees from a board of directors?

If we consider how boards actually determine what is reasonable for an investment adviser to earn, we find that the answer to this question is no. First, section 36(b) does not require that the board attempt to ensure that the adviser's fees in any sense replicate what a competitive market would produce. On the contrary, section 36(b) seems to assume that the adviser will charge the fund *more* than a competitive price, and the *Gartenberg* court specifically precluded a fund's directors from considering the fees and expenses of competing advisers. Underlying section 36(b), as well as the *Gartenberg* ruling, is the notion, noted earlier, that advisers have interests that conflict with those of the fund's shareholders, and that the adviser is not operating in a competitive market. As the court said in *Gartenberg*, "Competition between money market funds for shareholder business does not support an inference that competition must therefore also exist between adviser-managers for fund business. The former may be vigorous even though the latter is virtually non-existent. Each is governed by different forces. Reliance on prevailing industry advisory fees will not satisfy."[32]

This peculiar statement was essential to the court's analysis, and of a piece with the thinking that led to the adoption of section 36(b) in 1970. If the market for advisory services were in fact competitive, there would be no need for a board of directors to control the charges of the adviser, since the adviser would have to price its fees on a competitive basis. Section 36(b) seemed necessary to Congress because Congress was led to believe that prices were not set competitively in the mutual fund industry.

In any event, to make its judgments under section 36(b), the board receives data from the adviser that document the adviser's costs in providing various services to the fund. In addition to the advisory fee itself, these costs often include 12b-1 (distribution) fees, subadvisory services, and fees for other activities such as account maintenance, accounting and auditing, legal and administrative services, transfer agency and custodial services, and keeping books and records. After satisfying itself that the costs borne by the adviser for providing these services are within a reasonable range, and comparable to the costs of services that the adviser might purchase elsewhere, the board allows the adviser to charge the fund—as a reasonable profit—somewhat more than the adviser's costs.

This process creates an economic environment for the adviser's management that is entirely different from a fully competitive environment. In the latter, other advisers would be offering lower costs to attract investors, and—assuming that investors respond—this would require that higher-cost advisers lower their rates to meet the competition. They would be forced to find less expensive inputs in order to maintain their profitability, or perhaps even to survive. This is how competition increases efficiency and promotes innovation. The presence of a board of directors with power to determine what would be a reasonable profit, and to add that profit to the adviser's costs in setting fees, changes the calculus for advisers.

It may well be that an adviser could attract more investors by lowering its fees and costs, but if the adviser does that, and thereby succeeds in increasing its profit, the board may take that increased profit away in the next fee negotiation. Indeed, the common requirement that advisers establish breakpoints in their fee schedules—in order to recapture for the fund some of the benefits of an adviser's economies of scale—is a perfect illustration of Kahn's point that rate regulation reduces the regulated industry's incentive to operate more efficiently and thereby lower its costs.[33] Having taken the revenue risk associated with reducing its fees and expenses, the adviser discovers that it has to give back some or all of its resulting profit in the form of a breakpoint or two. This is a clear disincentive to reducing fees and expenses, making it rational for an adviser instead to maintain its expense ratio at a level that will not cause a reduction in profits at the next fee negotiation, but that is not so high as to chase away investors. When all investment advisers follow this course, the result is the mutual fund market we see today: all the normal indicators of competition are present, yet prices have not converged downward toward a common marginal cost.

Note that in this system neither the adviser nor the board is in any way at fault. Rather, highly motivated advisers and highly diligent boards are both caught in the process established by section 36(b) of the ICA, as explicated by *Gartenberg*, in which boards are required to regulate the adviser's profits just as utility commissions are required to regulate utility rates—and cannot in the process consider the prices of competitors. Once this regulatory process was established, it was foreordained that fund pricing would never converge to a single competitive price for similar services. That, in turn, means that the costs of investing in the average mutual fund will inevitably be higher than would prevail in a competitive market.

Our demonstration of the wide disparity in mutual fund expense ratios makes clear that boards of directors are not effective in controlling costs. This is entirely understandable and certainly not the result of any lack of independence. The only cost information that an adviser furnishes to a board of directors is information on average or fixed costs, not the marginal cost of providing the advisory service. In a competitive market, most economists believe, the marginal cost of the most efficient producer—that is, the cost to that producer of furnishing the last profitable unit of the product or service—sets, and should set, the market price.[34] All other competitors, if they wish to stay in business, must either differentiate themselves from the most efficient producer or match that price.

But the fund board cannot be expected to determine the marginal cost of the adviser and thus the price that the adviser would charge in a fully competitive market. Alfred Kahn again explains why:

> Manifestly, the operating expenses and capital outlays of public utility companies are by far the most important component of their rate levels.... Therefore, in terms of their quantitative importance, it would be reasonable to expect regulatory commissions to give these costs the major part of their attention. But in fact they have not done so; they have given their principal attention instead to the limitation of profits.
>
> The reasons for this perverse distribution of effort illustrate once again the inherent limitations of regulation as an institution of effective social control of industry. Effective regulation of operating expenses and capital outlays would require a detailed, day-by-day, transaction-by-transaction, and decision-by-decision review of every aspect of the company's operation. Commissions could do so only if they were prepared completely to duplicate the role of management itself.[35]

Kahn describes exactly what happens when a board of directors attempts to negotiate what should be the adviser's compensation for management services, and thus the adviser's price to investors in the fund. The board, as required by section 36(b), attempts to limit the adviser's profits, not to find the price for the adviser's services that would replicate a competitive price.

The investment adviser does not furnish marginal cost information to the board for two reasons. First, as noted above, the adviser has an incentive to furnish only average costs, because its profit is determined by reference to these costs, which typically are higher than marginal costs. Second, and perhaps more important, the adviser *does not know* what its marginal costs actually are, since these can only be determined in a competitive market. In a famous essay, "Competition as a Discovery Procedure," Friedrich Hayek pointed out that only through actual competition can one determine what a product or service might actually cost in a competitive environment.[36] This is because the most important facts—such as the price at which the last consumer will buy and the marginal cost of the last input— are not known and cannot be known in advance of actual competition. The costs of inputs keep changing, as does the price the last consumer is willing to pay for a given amount of a product or service. None of these things can be forecast or discovered in advance, and thus they cannot be communicated to boards of directors, even if investment advisers had an incentive to do so.

One other point is also important to note: at least some of the costs reported by advisers to boards must be arbitrarily determined. This is not because of any wish on the part of advisers to mislead fund boards, but simply because there is no right or rational way for any organization engaged in a joint enterprise—such as managing two or more mutual funds—to allocate certain costs between them. To take a simple example, how would an investment adviser that initially advises only one fund and later adds another allocate its investment research costs between the two? The new fund may at first take more time of the adviser's research staff than the old one, so does that mean that these costs should be allocated principally to the new fund? Perhaps, but the effect of this will be to substantially reduce the adviser's costs on the old fund, and perhaps require the board of the old fund to reduce the adviser's profit on that fund to a "reasonable" level under section 36(b). Once both funds are operating and start-up costs are no longer a factor, how should the adviser allocate its costs? If we assume that the new fund is half the size of the old, but the adviser's staff spends the same amount of time on each, should the adviser's personnel costs for the old fund be cut in half, or should the adviser allocate personnel costs so that each fund bears them in proportion to its size? Alternatively, the adviser could argue plausibly that the new fund was started principally to take advantage of the economies of scope associated with having two funds rather than one; for example, once the adviser is doing NAV calculations for one fund, it will not cost much more to do the same for two. In this view only the adviser's incremental costs should be allocated to the new fund.

None of these methods—and one can think of others—is obviously wrong, but they lead to entirely different results when the board comes to consider the adviser's compensation fund by fund. The obvious problem here is that the board cannot, under the language of section 36(b), review and pass upon the adviser's overall profits for both funds jointly, even though they are in fact managed jointly. Section 36(b) is based on the fiction that the board and the adviser have fiduciary responsibilities to the shareholders of each fund separately, and thus the board must review the adviser's compensation for each fund apart from the others.

Under these circumstances, advisers are inevitably led to allocate costs so as to produce "reasonable" profits where they want these profits to appear, and to produce lower profits, or losses, where they want these to appear. Most independent directors probably know this but permit this arrangement because compliance with the literal language of section 36(b) is impossible. As one expert in cost accounting noted in a book on the subject, "*All methods of allocating joint costs are arbitrary*. . . . Allocating joint costs poses issues for accountants because the needs of allocated joint costs for financial reporting differ from those for decision making. Cost accounting systems serve multiple purposes, including product pricing, product emphasis, cost control, and reporting to internal and external constituents. The same set of computations rarely satisfies every purpose" (emphasis in original).[37] The inherent arbitrariness of the cost allocation process, an essential element of the responsibilities laid on advisers and boards in negotiating fees and expenses, suggests that a new and different system for determining the fees and expenses of advisers is necessary—one that does away with the need for section 36(b) altogether.

The Vanguard Exception

Before we leave the subject of price formation among mutual funds, it is instructive to discuss one major exception to the general rule. The funds operated by the Vanguard Group are very often the lowest-cost funds in the industry. We believe the reason for this is the different organizational structure of Vanguard, which is organized as a mutual company instead of a corporation. As outlined below, we believe this structure creates a different set of incentives for the Vanguard adviser and trustees. Table 4-4 illustrates the disparity in expense ratios between Vanguard funds of different kinds and a range of competitors.

Like many insurance companies and a few remaining thrift institutions, Vanguard is organized in mutual rather than corporate form. The Vanguard *funds* jointly own the company that provides management services and serves as their investment adviser. Presumably the management company provides its advisory and other services at cost (recognizing the arbitrariness of this concept), including the salary and other compensation of the company's officers and employees. Since the management company is not a public company and all its shares are owned by the funds it advises, little is known about its compensation practices. However, it can be assumed that the company's managers do not accept compensation that is substantially lower than that paid to the managers of other mutual fund advisers. This might lead one to believe that the low expense ratios of the Vanguard funds reflect a lower cost of operations, arising out of its mutual structure, and that other investment advisory firms do not adopt this structure because they want to charge more than Vanguard for their services. This, however, is not likely to be the reason that Vanguard funds are able to keep their expense ratios lower than other fund managers.

As mutual insurance companies, savings and loan associations, stock exchanges, and credit unions have found, a mutual form of organization is a perfectly workable way to operate a business unless large amounts of capital are necessary for expansion—in which case a corporate form typically (but not always) seems to work best. Indeed, that is the reason why many mutual organizations—the New York Stock Exchange and NASDAQ are prominent examples—have recently converted to corporate form. However, the idea that the mutual form of organization is inherently

TABLE 4-4

EXPENSE RATIOS OF SELECTED VANGUARD FUNDS

AND COMPETITORS (percent)

Fund Style	Fund Name and Ticker Symbol	Expense Ratio
Domestic mid-cap growth	Vanguard Mid-Cap Growth (VMGRX)	0.39
	Pioneer Mid-Cap Growth A (PITHX)	0.90
	Fidelity Mid Cap Growth (FSMGX)	1.00
	Evergreen Mid Cap Growth A (EKAAX)	1.13
	BlackRock Mid Cap Growth Investor B (BMGBX)	2.33
Short-term government bond (taxable)	Vanguard Short-Term Treasury (VFISX)	0.26
	AIM Limited Maturity Treasury A (SHTIX)	0.60
	Merrill Lynch Short Term U.S. Government I (MAAJX)	0.66
	Morgan Stanley Limited Duration U.S. Treasury Trust (LDTRX)	0.82
	Putnam Limited Duration Government Income B (PBGBX)	1.64
Global equity	Vanguard Global Equity (VHGEX)	0.80
	Janus Global Opportunities (JGVAX)	1.02
	Oppenheimer Global Opportunities A (OPGIX)	1.16
	AIM Global Equity A (GTNDX)	1.50
	Seligman Global Growth A (SHGOX)	2.10
Money market	Vanguard Prime Money Market Fund (VMMXX)	0.30
	Fidelity Cash Reserves (FDRXX)	0.43
	Columbia Cash Reserves A (CPMXX)	0.65
	Evergreen Money Market Fund (EMAXX)	0.92
	Van Kampen Reserve Fund A (ACZXX)	0.97

SOURCES: Morningstar, www.morningstar.com (accessed July 20, 2006) and (for money market funds) fund literature.
NOTE: Data are as of July 20, 2006.

superior to the external management form—an idea widely promoted by the writings of John Bogle, Vanguard's founder[38]—is something of an overstatement.

The principal costs of an advisory and management function are personnel costs, and management companies of both organizational forms have to pay these. Although it is true that outside investment advisers also have to compensate their shareholders, this may not result in significant differences in actual returns to fund investors. Since the managers of mutual organizations cannot own shares in the enterprise, they may typically be compensated with higher salaries, or profit-sharing arrangements, so that the net return to the Vanguard fund shareholders may be no higher than it would be if the entire structure were in more conventional form. But even if the salary costs were somewhat lower, it is unlikely that this would save Vanguard's shareholders any more than a few basis points.

Nonetheless, one major difference between the Vanguard structure and the conventional corporate form is relevant to this analysis. The Vanguard structure eliminates the need for a board of directors to evaluate the costs of the adviser in order to establish the adviser's allowable fees and expenses. The board of trustees of each Vanguard fund can set the price for the fund's services—its fees and expenses—without reference to the investment adviser's costs. In other words, the trustees of Vanguard funds have an incentive to lower the fund's price (fees and expenses) if that will attract more investors, because the shareholders of the Vanguard funds are automatically the beneficiaries of the economies of scale that a larger fund produces. No recapture of these benefits is necessary.

Accordingly, the most significant source of the Vanguard funds' low expense ratios may be that their managements have a different set of incentives, and a more complete knowledge of the costs of managing the funds, in setting their prices. If so, the external managers of mutual funds structured in the more conventional way could be given the same incentives to lower their costs, and competition should then drive their expense ratios down to something like those that Vanguard exhibits today.

A natural question, of course, is, if Vanguard's model is so superior, why don't other funds copy it? The answer in part depends on the needs of the advisory organization, on the regulatory approvals that would be required, and on the incentives set up by the U.S. tax system. In general, companies that need capital to start up will find it easier to organize initially in a corporate rather than mutual form. In a mutual form, the first members of management must themselves advance the necessary funds to get the operation off the ground. As it happens, Vanguard started from an existing corporate structure and only later converted to a mutual form.[39] This was probably difficult, because once an operation is a going concern, conversion to a mutual form requires buying out the existing shareholders, and if, as in Vanguard's case, this is to be done by one or more mutual funds, a number of difficult regulatory hurdles must be crossed. In addition, compensation of the members of the management group may be tax advantaged in the corporate form, because the managers can receive restricted stock or stock options, which are taxed at a lower rate when realized than cash compensation. Yet, in simpler regulatory times, evidently Vanguard overcame all these obstacles.

Is Inadequate Disclosure the Problem?

Up to now we have seen why the mutual fund industry, despite a structure that should produce vigorous price competition that would substantially reduce investors' costs, has not done so. We have seen how the requirement under section 36(b) that boards of directors review advisers' fees and expenses places a limit on the advisers' incentive to reduce their costs. But why, these limitations notwithstanding, have investors themselves not flocked to the lowest-cost funds, thereby forcing higher-cost investment advisers to lower their fees and expenses as well?

Before turning to this question, it is necessary to dispose of one more false idea that turned up in the court's *Gartenberg* opinion. This is the notion that investors do not care about fees and expenses because they are such a small proportion of the benefits they receive from mutual fund performance. The *Gartenberg* court stated, "One reason why fund competition for shareholder business does not lead to competition between adviser-managers for fund business is the relative insignificance of the adviser's fee to each shareholder. The fund customer's shares [sic] of the advisory fee is usually too small a factor to lead him to invest in one fund rather than in another or to monitor adviser-manager's fees."[40]

This statement reflects a misunderstanding of how a competitive market in mutual funds would work. If advisers were able to compete on price, they would seek the last *marginal* investor. Those investors who do not in fact care about the small fees or expenses they pay, although perhaps the substantial majority of investors, are largely irrelevant for purposes of analyzing competition in the marketplace. Like profit-maximizing providers in any industry, what the adviser is looking for is the *last profitable investor*, the last investor whose contribution to revenue will exceed the marginal cost of advising that investor. This is literally textbook economics.[41] The relatively low cost of the adviser's services in relation to the benefits they produce is thus irrelevant, as is the observation that investors in general pay little attention to these costs. In a competitive market, advisers compete for the investors who *do* care, and it is these investors who determine the price. It is simply not credible, given the significant effect over the long term of high expense ratios, that at least some investors, and possibly a substantial number, would not respond to price competition. Our own survey found that a small number of respondents were well aware of what they were paying in advisory fees, and this suggests that competition for the business of even that small percentage would stimulate efficient operation and price reductions among advisory groups.

There are reasons why the vast majority of investors pay little attention to the prices charged by investment advisers. In the discussion above, we suggested that many investors may assume that the costs of mutual fund investment are broadly the same, just as they are in other areas of the economy where competition prevails. But there are other possibilities.

In its 2000 report on the mutual fund industry, the GAO proceeded on the assumption that the mutual fund industry exhibited "monopolistic competition" because disclosure to investors was inadequate.[42] The agency conducted a number of public surveys and interviewed industry participants, regulators, and academic and other observers. The report noted that, over the years, the SEC had required more disclosure by funds and better presentation of the information that was disclosed—first requiring a separate statement of expense ratios, then a fee table in prospectuses and annual reports summarizing the costs that the adviser was charging to the fund, and finally a statement of the dollar cost that any investor would bear on a hypothetical investment of $10,000 over one, three, five, and ten years. None of this apparently had the desired effect. According to the GAO, investors in general were still largely ignorant or unconcerned about advisers' costs. The agency reported:

> Even after purchasing shares, investors apparently continue to consider other factors ahead of fund fees when reviewing their mutual funds. A 1997 ICI report,[43] relating the results of interviews with over 1,000 recent mutual fund purchasers, selected at random, stated that 76 percent of those surveyed had considered fees and expenses before making their purchases. However, respondents cited five other factors, including account value and rate of return, as information they monitored more frequently than fees and expenses after they had made their purchases.
>
> The apparent lack of investors' attention to fees . . . has been a source of concern for regulators. During testimony before the House Subcommittee on Finance and Hazardous Materials of the Committee on Commerce, SEC's Chairman stated: "The Commission is very concerned . . . that many fund investors are not paying attention to the available information about fees." He further stated that the agency's research showed that fewer than one in six investors understood that higher expenses can lead to lower returns, and fewer than one in five could give any estimate of expenses for their largest mutual fund.[44]

This of course accords with the results of our own survey, described earlier in this chapter, which found that investors know very little about advisory fees or expense ratios or even how they are calculated. It seems clear that fees and expenses are just not on the radar screens of investors, even though over time they can have a significant effect on returns. The GAO noted:

> In the academic papers and speeches we reviewed and the interviews we conducted, observers agreed that . . . mutual funds do not compete primarily on the basis of their operating expense fees . . . . Instead . . . fund advisers generally emphasize the performance of their funds when attempting to differentiate their funds

from those of their competitors. . . . To document factors mutual fund companies emphasize in their promotions, we analyzed a selection of mutual fund print advertisements for content. We evaluated 43 mutual fund advertisements for 28 different mutual fund families, which appeared in 5 randomly selected issues of popular business, news, or personal finance magazines and 1 business newspaper between July and November 1999. In 27 of the 43 advertisements, performance was the primary emphasis; and attributes of the fund adviser, such as its experience or strategy, were primarily emphasized in another 11. Fees and other charges were the primary emphasis in 2 of the 43 advertisements, both of which were from the same fund family.[45]

Elsewhere in its discussion, the GAO pointed out that understanding the many factors that go into making a judgment about a fund can be daunting: ". . . [the] SEC Chairman has stated that investors are not paying attention to the available fee information. He voiced concern that the fee structures of some mutual funds are too complex, making it more difficult for investors to evaluate overall costs and services. In a 1998 speech to an ICI gathering, the chairman asked 'Do you really expect investors to understand alphabet soup of A, B, C, D, I, Y and Z shares? To figure what combination of front-end loads, CDSLs [contingent deferred sales loads], 12b-1 charges, commissions and who knows what else they are paying?'"[46]

In discussing fund advertising and the complexity of fund disclosures, the GAO was indeed on to something, but it did not follow through to consider the reasons for its findings. Ultimately, the GAO's recommendations were for yet more detailed disclosure—in this case the dollar costs to each investor, personalized to that investor's account—in the hope that this final additional bit of information suddenly would make investors sit up and take notice that they can increase their investment returns by moving their money from expensive funds to inexpensive ones. It is likely, however, that this idea, if ever actually adopted, will also fail, because it is based on an incomplete understanding of the reasons why funds and advisers compete only weakly on price.

Why, indeed, are funds' disclosures about fees and expenses so complicated? Is it just a coincidence that weak price competition, as discussed above, and a complicated form of disclosure exist in a market in which prices are regulated by boards of directors, or is there a relationship between the two?

In our foregoing discussion about the fee regulation process, we noted that investment advisers have weak to no incentives to lower their prices in order to attract additional business. If they take the risk of doing so, and actually succeed in attracting more investors, part of the profit associated with that risk—if the board of directors is diligent on behalf of the share-holders—will be promptly taken away in the form of new breakpoints (the term "recaptured" is occasionally used) at the next annual fee negotiation. Even were this not so, competing by lowering fees and expenses would reduce the profits of the external adviser, because inevitably, like public util-ity commissions, boards of directors treat the profit element as an allowance over and above the costs that the adviser reports to them.

Similarly, in their presentations to boards of directors, advisers are likely to structure their cost disclosures so as to make the presentation most com-pelling, and in conformity with the way the adviser accounts for its costs internally. This results in a highly complex welter of different costs for the many services the adviser performs for the fund—costs that, moreover, are not uniformly presented across funds because the ways advisers run their businesses and allocate their costs are not uniform. So what we see in mutual fund fee and expense disclosures is far more complex than would occur in a competitive market, where the objective of competitors is to simplify their pricing so as to make it more understandable and attractive to consumers.

In short, both the fees and expenses themselves and the way that invest-ment advisers present them are an artifact of the regulatory process through which they must pass under the ICA. And investors, in turn, do not respond to high fees and expenses, using these as important factors in deciding where to invest, because the funds and fund families themselves do not ask them to make their investment decisions on this basis or make it easy for them to compare one fund with another price. As the GAO found in its survey, advis-ers do not advertise their wares this way; instead they focus the attention of investors on features other than price that may more readily distinguish one fund from another. They do not advertise their prices because—for the rea-sons outlined in detail above—they have very little incentive to make low prices a basis on which an investor should make an investment choice. The benefit that comes from lowering prices simply does not justify the potential cost. Indeed, advertising lower fees and expenses, from the perspective of the adviser that has to give back a portion, if not all, of the gain from such advertising, would just throw good money after bad.

In the rest of the economy, firms advertise for business by drawing the attention of consumers to the special qualities of their products and services. The purpose of advertising is twofold: to make consumers aware of a product, and to reduce their search costs—as economists call them—in finding the distinguishing features of the product that will induce a purchase. Consumers rarely take the time to discover on their own the special qualities that distinguish one product from another. It's too much time and trouble. Instead advertisers try to do that for them. So, if firms in a given industry have little incentive to lower prices, they will not ask potential consumers to make investment judgments on the basis of lower prices.

This suggests that, to improve pricing for mutual fund investors, it is necessary to introduce price competition into the collective investment market, *and that requires a thoroughgoing change in its regulatory structure.* When investment advisers and fund families have an incentive to lower their fees and expenses, *and* to call those lower fees and expenses to the attention of investors, investors will begin to see real reductions in prices.

Earlier Efforts to Promote Competition— The SEC's Division of Investment Management and the UFIC

As we have argued so far, the best, if not the only, way to bring competition, risk taking, and lower fees and expenses to the mutual fund industry is to eliminate the rate regulation now carried on by the boards of directors of mutual funds. This is not a new idea. As early as 1980, Stephen K. West, a well-known lawyer and expert in mutual fund regulation, proposed a radical change in the regulation of mutual funds. West's idea was to amend the ICA to permit the creation of a new collective investment structure that he called a unitary investment fund, or UIF. West further explicated this idea in an extensive report for the Investment Company Institute in 1990, summarizing it as follows: "The structure discussed here as a possibility is a contract type entity which is *not* independent of its sponsor or manager. In fact its very form reflects its nature as a proprietary financial product being continually offered to the public. Its design and operation and its success or failure is [sic] entirely the responsibility of its sponsor/manager. The investors relate to or are connected with the sponsor/manager."[47] As noted in chapter 2, West's UIF idea was picked up by the SEC in 1982 and embodied in a concept release, but went no further.

The UIF as proposed by West would have been an optional form of contractual relationship between an investment adviser and investors. There would be no intervening corporate entity and no board of directors. The investment adviser would manage a pooled fund consisting of the contributions of many investors for an "all-in" fee that could not be changed without investor approval or advance notice. As outlined in his 1990 report, West saw several advantages in this structure: ". . . the elimination of large amounts of administrative work at the state and federal level involved with the corporate governance structure, to say nothing of the internal administration and legal work involved . . . [and] the working out of a reciprocal arrangement for the cross border sale of United States funds and UCITS type funds now permitted throughout the EC."[48]

In its 1992 report, *Protecting Investors: A Half Century of Investment Company Regulation*, the SEC's Division of Investment Management considered the UIF proposal, noting that it is "predicated on the belief that an investment company is a proprietary product, more suited to a contractual arrangement than to corporate democracy. Its advocates claim that the UIF's simplified governance and fee arrangements would be more flexible for the manager and comprehensible to investors."[49] In its analysis, the Division saw value in eliminating rate regulation by the board of directors, but saw no alternative to retaining a board of directors to deal with conflicts of interest between the adviser and the fund: "We conclude that, although the UIF's approach to fees generally is sound and should be implemented with minor modifications, there is no practical substitute for the oversight of boards of directors regarding investment company operations."[50]

Accordingly, in the same report, the SEC staff endorsed a revised version of the UIF, which it called the unified fee investment company, or UFIC.[51] The principal difference between the UIF and the UFIC was that the latter retained the corporate form, with a board of directors responsible for policing conflicts of interest between the shareholders and the investment adviser, but was no longer involved in passing upon the adviser's fees or expenses unless they were "unconscionable or grossly excessive."

The staff's rationale for endorsing the fixed, unified fee and the free movement of shareholders recognized the importance of a single price in stimulating competition among mutual funds: "[T]he Division has concluded that a new type of open-end investment company that has readily determinable and comparable expenses and minimal barriers to exit . . . would appeal to investors because of the simplicity of its fee and would *foster competitive pricing among bond and stock funds.* Accordingly, the Division recommends that the Commission propose amendments to the Act to permit the UFIC, an alternative type of mutual fund with a single fee" (emphasis added).[52]

The UFIC proposal was advanced to Congress by the SEC, in legislation cosponsored by Congressmen Jack Fields (R-TX) and Edward J. Markey (D-MA) in 1995 as H.R. 1495. The bill would have authorized the SEC to exempt a registered open-end investment company from specified statutory prescriptions, including breach of fiduciary duty; required the manager to pay all expenses of such a fund out of a single all-in management fee; required that the board of directors of the exempted company be composed of persons at least two-thirds of whom were independent directors; and designated the exempted company as a unified fee investment company. One hearing was held in a subcommittee, but no further action was taken.

Although the Division did not explain in detail the reasons for believing that a single fee, established by an adviser and not subject to approval by the board of directors of a fund, would foster competitive pricing, its rationale appears to have been that the simplicity of a single, unified fee would permit investors to compare funds more easily.[53] In its discussion of the UFIC, the Division outlined a number of conditions associated with this new structure:

- The UFIC would not be a substitute for the conventional mutual fund form, but simply a legislatively authorized alternative.

- A written management contract between the investment manager and the UFIC would specify a single, unified fee for all the manager's services to the fund.

- UFIC investors would not be charged front-end loads or redemption fees, and no 12b-1 fees would be assessed to the fund for distribution.

- UFIC shareholders would not vote on issues related to fees or contracts.

- The manager could not use fund brokerage or free credit balances of the fund to pay for services, but brokerage costs would be charged to the fund.

- The manager could change the fee on ninety days' notice to the shareholders, who would then have the opportunity to redeem their shares without cost.

- Section 36(b) would not apply to the manager of a UFIC or the manager's affiliates.

- A board of directors would continue to monitor the adviser's performance and conflicts of interest between the adviser and the shareholders.

The Division's endorsement of the UFIC idea reflected a major change in the attitude of the SEC's staff (at least at the time) about the effectiveness of regulation in protecting investors: "We do not believe that the UFIC's investors need the protections of the defensive procedures generally followed by investment company boards to ensure compliance with section 36(b). The UFIC would have few barriers to competitive pricing, so that competition could be substituted for regulation. Its key features—a readily determinable single fee and minimal exit barriers—would permit the UFIC to be freed from the regulatory restraint of Section 36(b), imposed to compensate for the limited competition that was ineffectual in restraining fee levels."[54]

It should not surprise readers to learn, by this point, that we find a lot in the Division's proposal that makes sense. We have stated our belief that the need for board approval of advisory fees and expenses is responsible for the lack of vigorous price competition among mutual funds today. In our view, if advisers were free (or required) to set a single all-in rate for their services, that would—as the Division seemed to believe in 1992—finally open up to investors the advantages of the vigorous price competition that has taken place in every market where deregulation has occurred in recent years.[55] We would also agree with the Division's suggestion that there should be no or very little limitation on the freedom of investors to move from fund to fund in response to price improvements or other factors, and that all marketing expenses should come out of the adviser's fee and not the assets of the fund. In addition, laws or regulations that forbid advisers from using affiliates for fund brokerage, or any other service paid for out of fund assets rather than the adviser's all-in fee, would seem appropriate. Certainly, there would be no further reason for section 36(b), since the underlying concept of this aspect of the UFIC is to treat the adviser as a service provider in a competitive market rather than as a fiduciary. The adviser's prices—as the Division itself suggested—would be disciplined by competition in the market, not by regulation. Finally, any new structure should be optional, so that investors who like their existing fund relationships or are satisfied with fee-regulating boards of directors can retain them.

These are the central ideas underlying the UFIC as outlined by the Division. Insofar as it would reduce fees and expenses to investors by eliminating board approval and encouraging vigorous competition, we endorse it as a major improvement in the structure of the collective investment market in the United States. Accordingly, in the balance of this discussion, we will refer to the Division's proposal as the UFIC idea—the name adopted by the Division—even though we will recommend in the next chapter major changes in the structure the Division had in mind.

However, the immediate question raised by the UFIC structure, as conceived by the Division, is this: if the fund board of directors is no longer charged with the responsibility for overseeing the adviser's fees and expenses, and if the other reforms suggested by the Division in the UFIC are adopted, is there any longer a need for a board to deal with conflicts of interest? Put another way, assuming that some conflicts remain, is a board of directors the best and most efficient way to address them?

The Division in the 1990s continued to see a role for a board of directors as part of the UFIC proposal: "Except as to fee issues, a UFIC generally would have the same types of operational conflicts and potential for overreaching by management that inhere in the structure of open-end investment companies." This, in the Division's view, would justify continuing the UFIC as a corporate form with a board of directors charged with protecting the shareholders against the conflicting interests of the adviser. What conflicts did the Division have in mind? The Division suggested that an adviser might be tempted to "skimp on the basic level of services" to the fund in order to keep more of the unitary fee for itself, or might "hire an incompetent custodian."[56] To address this problem, the Division recommended that the directors have the authority to terminate the advisory contract and any service contract that the adviser might enter into, even though the adviser would now be using only its own funds—coming from the unitary fee—to pay for these services.

In light of this comment, we find it difficult to take seriously the Division's rationale for retaining a board or eliminating its fee-setting role. After concluding that competition among advisers, based on a single all-in or unitary fee, would be an adequate substitute for regulation and provide a basis for eliminating section 36(b), the Division here simply reintroduced director management and price regulation by the back door. Although it is unlikely that the board would ever terminate the advisory contract—for the simple reason that the investors and not the board chose this adviser when they bought shares in the fund—it is certainly possible that the board would countermand the adviser's judgment in choosing a custodian or a transfer agent or any of the many other service providers for a fund. Since the purpose of the unitary fee is to force advisers to compete, and thus drive down fund expenses, this idea defeats the purpose. If an adviser's fee, like that of any other general contractor, is built on the costs of its subcontracts, the board's ability to terminate the subcontracts and insist, for example, on more expensive services vitiates the adviser's ability to establish a firm price on the basis of which it can compete with others.

Moreover, it is difficult to imagine how the independent directors, or anyone else who is not a professional appraiser, would be able to judge the value of the services performed under contract with the adviser, or why they should. In every other aspect of their interaction with a competitive market, consumers are called upon to evaluate the interrelationship of price and service. If they want additional services, they are obliged to pay for them. For some reason, however, this is considered inappropriate or impossible for the same consumers when they become mutual fund investors. In support of its position, the Division offers the lame excuse that investors "lack the expertise or incentive to assess the quality and level of fund services."[57] But if the Division really believes this, there is no point in opening the market to price competition through the UFIC structure. If investors are that helpless, they will also be unable to determine whether they will be getting value for the adviser's all-in fee.

Finally, in concept the Division's analysis here seems to go back to the discredited idea about "destructive competition" that was used to justify some government regulation early in the twentieth century and in the ICA. However, earlier in the same chapter of the 1992 report, the Division recommends eliminating section 22(d), a resale price maintenance provision, because it impairs competition. In support of its position, the Division cites the following statement by the Justice Department in 1973: "The Supreme Court has noted that ruinous competition, financial disaster, evils of price cutting, and the like appear throughout our history as ostensible, albeit unpersuasive, justifications for price-fixing."[58] In citing, in its discussion of UFICs, the possibility that competition might induce investment advisers to cut corners—in other words, engage in "ruinous competition"—the Division is contradicting a view it supported only a few pages earlier.

The ironic thing about the Division's argument citing the potential evils of competition—as with many of the other justifications advanced for retaining a corporate form and board of directors—is that it is so out of phase with the rest of U.S. securities law. The Securities Act of 1933 and the Securities Exchange Act of 1934 are based on the idea that individuals can make securities selections on their own if provided with adequate information and a fair market. Although many academics doubt that it is possible for anyone to beat the market over the long term, the SEC makes every effort in administering the 1933 and 1934 acts to give investors confidence that they can make choices among issuers by rational analysis of the facts that companies are required to disclose.

Still, investing in securities—as the Enron and WorldCom cases show—can be very risky. The "facts" sometimes turn out to be wrong, manipulated, or hard to interpret. One way to reduce these risks is to diversify—the very benefit among all others that mutual funds offer to investors. Although many students of the financial markets are indeed skeptical that even professional portfolio managers can outperform the stock market for long, there is no doubt that, by offering diversification, mutual funds reduce the risks of investing in stocks. Thus it is supremely ironic that the protection of a board of directors should be considered necessary for investors when they are making a relatively safe investment in a mutual fund, but not when they are encouraged to make nondiversified investments on their own. As we discuss in the next chapter, however, if investors need protection there are better ways to provide it than a board of directors.

5

The Managed Investment Trust Option

The UFIC idea discussed in chapter 4 was a major step forward for the SEC's Division of Investment Management. It reflected a recognition that the current system of pricing in the mutual fund industry, in which a board of directors approves the fees and expenses of the investment adviser, could be improved by allowing advisers to establish their own all-in fee and freeing investors to leave the fund at any time, without cost, if dissatisfied with the adviser's performance. The Division's idea was that the all-in fee would encourage vigorous price competition among funds and fund families, removing the need for the fund board of directors to review the adviser's fee setting. We agree. Our principal point in chapter 4 was that director approval of investment advisory fees and expenses impairs such competition.

But so far the SEC has not embraced the implications of the Division's logic in its 1992 report. It clings to its traditional and, we believe, incorrect view that the board of directors of a mutual fund—and particularly the independent directors—must be empowered to negotiate with the adviser over fees. While recommending that the board no longer control the adviser's fees and expenses, the Division saw "no alternative" to retaining a board of directors to address the adviser's "conflicts of interest." But there are alternatives. In our view, once the board is no longer called upon to approve something as important and consequential as the adviser's fee and expenses, it is no longer a cost-effective mechanism for dealing with the few potential conflicts of interest that remain.

In this concluding chapter we advance what we believe is a better solution than a fee-setting board of directors, and one more consistent with the Division's UFIC idea: permitting the development of a form of collective investment fund in which investors contract directly with the investment adviser without the intercession of a corporation or a board of directors. A contract structure of this kind is currently the dominant form of collective investment in most developed countries, including Canada, Japan, the United Kingdom, and most other countries of the European Union. In the few cases in these or other jurisdictions where there is a parallel or alternative corporate structure, it does not include a board of directors that is independent in any sense from the investment adviser.[1] Many of these contractual arrangements do involve an independent third party that oversees the activities of the investment adviser, but this is usually a trustee-custodian, not a board. In the contract structure, the focus of regulation is the adviser; the fund itself is not regulated and in general has no legal personality. It is usually a completely passive repository, controlled by a trustee, with the portfolio managed by an investment adviser.

A contract structure would not be completely foreign to the ICA; section 26 actually authorizes such a structure, which it refers to as a unit investment trust. The UIT is organized, in effect, as a contractual relationship between a trustee and investors. The relationship is governed by a trust indenture; there is no board of directors. The units of investment in the UIT represent an undivided interest in a pool of securities and may not be redeemable. However, if the units are not redeemable, the sponsor of the UIT usually maintains a market in the units, so that investors can liquidate their interests without depleting the trust.

The advantage of the UIT is that it offers diversification without the cost of an investment adviser; its disadvantage is that it is not actively managed and thus cannot change its portfolio as market conditions change. Our proposal is to create an alternative collective investment vehicle that is similar to the UIT but is actively managed and has redeemable units: what we call a managed investment trust, or MIT.

The MIT Model: Some Details

In the standard UIT arrangement, a securities firm, acting as a sponsor, assembles a pool of securities, deposits it in a trust organized under a trust indenture, and sells units in the pool to investors. Although an MIT would probably have to be structured somewhat differently, the basic UIT arrangement would be preserved. The MIT sponsor would be selling advisory services, not securities, although for technical reasons the units in the trust would be considered securities, which must be registered under the Securities Act of 1933.

The process would begin when a sponsor, probably an investment advisory firm, establishes a trust arrangement with a bank under an indenture that specifies all the obligations of the trustee and the sponsor-adviser. The sponsor-adviser would then offer subscriptions to redeemable units in the pool. The key element of the offer would be the sponsor's commitment to manage the pool's investments for a single, all-in fee as provided in the UFIC proposal. Subscribing investors would deposit their funds directly with the bank trustee. The trust agreement would not take effect until the pool had reached a predetermined size, sufficient for the MIT to be operated profitably.

The trust indenture, a standard document in any trust arrangement, would provide that the trustee, the owner of record of the trust assets, would take instructions from the adviser as to the buying and selling of the securities in the trust. The indenture would also specify that both the adviser and the trustee have fiduciary obligations to the investors, and that the trustee has the further obligation to oversee the compliance of the adviser with:

- the provisions of the trust indenture, including the trust's investment policy and limitations;

- the requirements of the ICA and the regulations issued under that law; and

- any other specific commitments made to the investors through the indenture or in the offering documents.

The fiduciary obligations of both the adviser and the trustee would be enforceable by the investors as well as by the SEC. The trustee also would function as the registrar and transfer agent of units in the pool and as custodian of the trust's assets. The fees of the trustee—probably a few basis points on the trust's assets—would be payable out of the all-in fee of the adviser.

In general, all the costs of operating the fund should be paid from the adviser's all-in fee. This would eliminate the adviser's temptation to structure its activities so as to place some of the costs of operating the fund on the fund itself—the source of the most serious potential conflicts of interest. The usual exceptions to this rule are brokerage fees, 12b-1 fees, and legal fees. All 12b-1 fees should certainly be eliminated, since the adviser would now be allowed to keep whatever profits come from attracting more investors. Legal fees should also be paid out of the adviser's fee. A trust is not a legal person and as such is not regulated; the adviser would be the regulated entity. The defendant in any suit would be the adviser or the trustee, and each should pay its own legal fees except as provided in the indemnification arrangements in the trust indenture. The change in structure and the inapplicability of section 36(b) should substantially reduce the legal liabilities of advisers, and insurance against any remaining liabilities should be available. Finally, consideration should be given to including brokerage fees in the all-in fee. If these three expenses were included in the all-in fee, and if the fee were set competitively, it would place all competitors on an equal footing, force advisers to determine how much of their profit they want to spend on distribution, and solve the problem of "soft dollar" compensation for advisers.[2]

In conformity with the underlying principles of the original UFIC idea, there should be no or minimal restrictions on the ability of investors to redeem their interests and exit the trust. Later in this chapter, we discuss mechanisms for reducing the obstacles that now limit the ability of investors to move from one fund to another.

The proposed MIT is similar to the unitary investment fund (UIF) proposed by Stephen West in 1980 and to the UFIC structure proposed by the SEC Division of Investment Management in its 1992 report. However, there are a number of important differences between the UIF and the MIT:

- Under the UIF, the adviser's all-in fee would be capped at an amount set by the SEC. We see no reason for a cap. As described in the Division's 1992 report, the all-in fee would encourage the development of a competitive market, which would in turn place a limit on the investment adviser's revenue commensurate with the expenses the adviser would be required to bear. Placing a cap on the all-in fee, or allowing the cap to be set by the SEC, would defeat the purpose and value of a competitively set fee.

- The indenture describing the UIF structure could not be modified for a five-year period. Further, in keeping with the concept underlying the UFIC, which relies on the ability of investors to move their funds with limited friction, we propose a ninety-day notice period before any substantial change in the indenture comes into effect, giving investors time to redeem their units and invest elsewhere.

- The UIF proposal contemplated no independent oversight of the activities of the adviser. In the MIT, as outlined more fully below, the depository bank, acting as a trustee for the investors, would have the responsibility of overseeing the actions of the adviser in managing the trust's assets.

Monitoring the MIT

The Division rejected the UIF proposal in 1992 because it believed a board of directors was necessary to control the adviser's conflicts of interest. We think this was a mistake. Eliminating the corporate form does not necessarily mean eliminating all independent checks on the adviser's activities. In other countries, methods have been developed that provide such independent oversight, even though the relationship between adviser and investor is contractual rather than corporate in form. In fact, these methods have the potential to achieve their purpose more efficiently and effectively than a board of directors. The structure used in the United Kingdom is particularly interesting in this respect, because it employs certain common law relationships that are familiar to Americans.

In the U.K. collective investment structure, collective investment funds can be organized either as corporations or as contractual relationships between an investor and an adviser. Both function in essentially the same way. In the contractual form, the investor contracts directly with the investment adviser for collective investment services. The manager deposits the investor's funds in a trust, managed by an independent trustee bank. The investor is a beneficiary of the trust and has a proportionate undivided interest in the trust corpus, represented by a certain number of units. The trust has no independent legal existence, so the depository bank is the legal owner of the funds the investors contribute and of the assets purchased with those funds. In addition to functioning as custodian of the trust's assets, the depository bank maintains the record of the investors' unit interests.

In this structure the depository (trustee) bank has the responsibility for overseeing the activities of the adviser in its management of the funds in the trust. We believe this approach can be adapted to work well in the contractual MIT structure. In our view the use of the bank to monitor and oversee the adviser's activities, and in appropriate cases to address the adviser's potential conflicts of interest, not only will be less expensive than a board of directors, thus permitting a higher return for investors, but also has the potential to perform the oversight and monitoring function more effectively.

In the United Kingdom both the depository bank and the investment adviser have fiduciary obligations to the investor. In a recent publication of the Investment Management Association, the trade organization of investment managers and advisers in the United Kingdom, the fiduciary obligation of the investment manager is described in part as follows: "[A] fiduciary must always act to secure the beneficiaries' best interests and must not allow its own interests to affect its behavior in any way that would conflict with the best interests of the beneficiaries."[3] Accordingly, fiduciary obligations in the United Kingdom are similar if not identical to those in the United States.

The United Kingdom also has a corporate form of collective investment fund. The investor buys shares of the corporation, and these funds are again deposited with a bank trustee. Although the corporation, unlike the trust, does have an independent legal existence, this does not appear to have any practical legal effect, because the investment manager can be the sole director of the corporation and has fiduciary duties to the shareholders that are essentially equivalent to the duties of a corporate director. For some reason, the fiduciary duties of the director in a U.K. fund have not been used to generate an adverse relationship between the adviser and the board or the shareholders. That might have been the case in the United States if Congress had made clear in the ICA that the adviser was intended to control the corporation through choosing its board of directors. The presence and responsibilities of independent directors in the ICA, in the absence of any clear contrary directions from Congress, left open the possibility that the board and the adviser were to be adverse.

Under both the trust and the corporate forms in the United Kingdom, the investment manager has sole control over the daily activities in the fund's portfolio, but the depository bank takes and gives up custody of shares bought and sold by the adviser. This is a key point; although it has no responsibility for setting or reviewing the advisory fee paid by the fund, the depository bank, as trustee, is responsible for overseeing the decisions and actions of the adviser, on a daily basis, from the standpoint of the investors' interests. Unlike a board of directors, the depository bank will have a professional staff devoted to this oversight function, and it will be performed on a daily and continuous basis, not quarterly or bimonthly, as is the case with the board of directors of a mutual fund. At one of the AEI conferences held as part of this research project, the president of the Investment Management Association reported that U.K. depository banks performed this function for an annual fee of 2 or 3 basis points, although a similar structure in the United States might, of course, be more costly.[4]

The U.K. structure could—indeed, should—work in the United States. Because the relevant legal concepts in the two countries are similar, a U.S. bank with a trust department could easily perform the functions now carried out by U.K. depository banks. The U.S. bank would have a fiduciary responsibility to the trust beneficiaries, which the beneficiaries could enforce under ordinary trust law in much the same way that directors of a fund are held liable to its shareholders.

The fact that the depository bank will have a professional staff to monitor the adviser's activities is key to our proposal. The use of bank staff for monitoring would be a major improvement on the monitoring abilities of a board of directors. A professional staff will be expert in understanding the requirements of the law and regulations applicable to the MIT, as well as the specific obligations that the investment manager has assumed in the offering documents for the MIT. And since it will have the fiduciary responsibilities of a trustee under U.S. trust law, the depository bank will have a strong incentive to be diligent in overseeing the adviser.

Moreover, because the depository bank would be a professional organization engaged in the business of overseeing funds, it would have more at stake than the independent directors of a fund in overseeing the activities of the adviser. As a professional organization, the bank trustee will be held to a higher standard than a board of directors, and failure to perform adequately could endanger a line of business. This is not to say, of course, that independent directors are not diligent; most are genuinely focused on improving the returns to investors and otherwise protecting the investors' interests. But in most cases they are employed elsewhere, are only engaged part-time, are not professionals in their role, and are not compensated in proportion to the time and attention they devote to their oversight activities.

Indeed, unlike a board of directors, which meets quarterly or bimonthly to perform its functions, the professional staff of the depository bank would deal with the adviser on a daily basis. Because the bank would be constantly receiving and disposing of assets held in trust as the adviser buys and sells securities, bank staff would be privy to a great deal of low-cost information about the adviser that would be useful in the bank's monitoring role. That the depository bank would have a permanent professional staff is particularly important, since part-time boards of directors simply cannot be expected to deal effectively with fifty or more different mutual funds in two-day meetings two or three months apart.[5] The existence of a professional staff with fiduciary obligations and constant contact with the adviser would seem especially well suited to one particular supervisory role—that of determining whether the adviser is taking excessive risks—for which boards of directors are not well equipped in terms of either time or technical expertise.

A particularly apt example of how the depository bank might be more effective than a board of directors is provided by the recent scandals involving late trading and market timing. In both cases, as discussed in detail in chapter 2, a number of advisers profited by allowing certain investors to engage in late-trading and market timing transactions. The boards of directors of the affected funds knew nothing of these arrangements and had no way to discover them because they had no access to what was happening at the adviser's level. However, because the depository bank would also function as the transfer agent for investors' interests in the trust, it could detect any such activity, and as a fiduciary it would be obliged to refuse to accommodate it.

As trustee, the depository also could be given authority, currently exercised by fund boards of directors, to propose remedies in the event that the adviser makes a negligent error of some kind in the administration of its functions. For relatively minor errors not requiring consultation with the SEC, the depository should be able to negotiate a settlement with the adviser in its capacity as trustee for those investors who might have been injured.

All told, a depository arrangement almost certainly would be less expensive than the current oversight system requiring a board of directors, since it would do away with such things as directors' fees, directors' meeting expenses, annual meetings of shareholders, proxy solicitations, directors' liability insurance, and the extensive management time required of the investment adviser to bring the directors up to date on the fund's operations and otherwise assure their good will. As noted above, the fee that banks in the United Kingdom charge for the oversight and monitoring services they perform has been reported to be 2 or 3 basis points on the assets of the trusts (on funds that are on average one-fifth the size of U.S. funds), although the services required under an MIT might be more extensive and might cost somewhat more.

To summarize, an MIT—a contractual relationship between an adviser and investors, combined with a trust indenture—not only would stimulate competition among advisers, driving down fees and expenses for investors. It would also provide a more effective system for monitoring the conflicts of interest that many believe are inherent in a collective investment structure.

Addressing Conflicts of Interest without a Board

In most discussions of conflicts of interest between an investment adviser and the shareholders of a mutual fund, there is little effort to consider what these conflicts actually are and whether there are alternative ways of addressing them. Here we will try to catalogue these conflicts and consider whether each can be addressed more effectively in some other way, particularly by a bank trustee functioning as such trustees currently do in the United Kingdom.

Clearly, the most serious conflicts arise in determining the adviser's fee and the other expenses of the adviser's operation of the fund. We believe we have addressed this set of conflicts by requiring that the adviser's all-in fee cover almost all fund expenses. If the all-in fee is set competitively, advisers will have every incentive to operate efficiently and keep their expenses low. The argument that this will result in skimping on services is rebutted by the extensive experience with competition in deregulated industries. In these industries—securities brokerage, trucking, and telecommunications, to name a few—rates have fallen substantially, yet services have improved or remained the same.[6]

Once a fund's board of directors is no longer engaged in approving the adviser's fees and expenses, the remaining conflicts of interest are relatively minor and fall into one of two classes. First, are those matters that are explicitly within the statutory authority of the board of directors or have been committed to the board, or to the independent directors alone, by SEC regulations. These include:

- statutory obligations to choose the company's independent auditors, oversee securities transactions involving affiliates to the extent permitted by the ICA, and approve joint liability insurance policies and fidelity bonds;

- regulatory duties to value certain types of portfolio securities, set the time of day when NAV is determined, approve mergers with other funds in the same family, approve custody contracts, determine the credit quality of debt securities in certain cases, and approve the investment company's code of ethics;

- duties to oversee the fair pricing of securities for which there is no readily available market value, ensure that appropriate procedures are established for the daily pricing of securities, approve the purchase of securities from an affiliated underwriter, and approve reverse repurchase agreements and the purchase or use of derivatives.

A second class of conflicts consists of those that have been identified over time as potential problems arising out of the relationship between the adviser and the fund. Some of these have actually occurred. Many, however, are speculative, and the possibility that they could occur has been cited as a basis for requiring a continuing role for a board of directors. A list of the most significant of these conflicts would include the following:[7]

- The adviser, in order to boost the fund's performance, may have an incentive to take greater investment risks than the investors expect.

- The allocation of brokerage services contracted by the fund may indirectly benefit the adviser, either through the use of an affiliated broker or through the receipt of additional compensation from the broker in "soft dollars," allocations of lucrative securities, or otherwise.

- The adviser may obtain additional or indirect compensation by "parking" the fund's assets with a bank that then compensates the adviser with a lower interest rate for an unrelated transaction. A variation of this is receiving parked funds in exchange for allowing late-trading.

- The adviser may have to allocate scarce securities among a number of funds, and this must be done on a fair and reasonable basis.

The Investment Adviser's Fiduciary Duty. Before turning to how these conflicts might be addressed without a board, it should be recalled that investment advisers have a fiduciary obligation to advisory customers. Although the Investment Advisers Act of 1940 does not explicitly impose such a duty, in *SEC v. Capital Gains Research Bureau, Inc.*, the Supreme Court indicated that an adviser is to be held to a fiduciary standard: "The Investment Advisers Act of 1940 . . . reflects a congressional recognition 'of the delicate fiduciary nature of an investment advisory relationship', as well as a congressional intent to eliminate or at least to expose, all conflicts of interest which might incline an investment adviser—consciously or unconsciously—to render advice which was not disinterested."[8] Thus, some protection of investors comes from the adviser's own fiduciary obligations.

The Value of the All-In Fee. As noted above, one way to reduce the need for extensive policing of conflicts of interest is to require that the adviser's all-in fee cover many of the items that formerly required the approval of the fund's board of directors. If the MIT structure induces competition among investment advisers, that itself will keep these fees under control and generally lower than they would be if approved and paid separately by each fund. For example, if the all-in fee were required to cover necessary joint liability insurance policies and fidelity bonds, there would be no further need for board approval, and the adviser would have an incentive to keep these fees as low as possible.

The same general analysis applies to contracts with the custodian of the fund's assets and with the transfer agent for trust units or other interests in the MIT. In the MIT format, custodial and transfer agency services would be performed by the trustee bank and included in the adviser's all-in fee. Under these circumstances the adviser would have every incentive to acquire these services at the lowest possible cost—a point fully consistent with the underlying rationale of the Division's UFIC idea. We assume, then, that the fee of the depository bank, which will perform custodial, transfer, and trustee services, will also be set competitively, since that fee will be paid out of the adviser's all-in fee. Competition for the business of advisers should cause banks that want to perform this role to seek efficient ways to do so, again improving investors' returns.

Similarly, up to now the independent auditors of mutual funds have been chosen by the directors of the funds, and their fees have been paid by the funds. Under the MIT structure, we would expect that the independent auditors for the trust will be chosen by the depository bank and—following the spirit of reducing conflicts of interest by requiring all-in fees—paid out of the bank's fees, not the trust's assets. Since the fees of the depository bank would be paid by the adviser, the auditors' fees would come indirectly out of the advisory fee.

Routine Activities. The only reason to place a particular decision in the hands of a fund's board or its independent directors rather than some other person or entity not affiliated with the adviser is to make use of their judgment in business matters. For the most part, the members of boards of directors—and especially the independent directors—are not likely to be specialists or experts in collective investment management; what they bring to the policing of conflicts of interest is common sense and sound business judgment. There is no point, then, in giving them assignments that do not call for these things. As the SEC's Division of Investment Management stated in its 1992 report, "[T]he Division recommends eliminating provisions in certain rules under the Act that make independent directors responsible for detailed findings of fact or for reviews and findings that involve more ritual than substance. Elimination of such formalistic requirements will increase the effectiveness of boards of directors by allowing them to focus to a greater extent on what they do best— exercising business judgment in their review of interested party transactions and in their oversight of operational matters where the interests of an investment company and its adviser diverge."9

However, many of the roles delegated to the board of directors by the ICA are either relatively routine and do not require business judgment, or are more suitable for determination by a technically skilled professional staff. In this category we would place valuing certain types of portfolio securities, setting the time of day when NAV is determined, approving custody contracts, determining the credit quality of debt securities, and approving a code of ethics. To the extent that any of these activities require independent review of an investment adviser's decision, they could be handled more effectively by the professional staff of a trustee depository bank than by a board of directors.

Violations That the Board Cannot Discover. Another important issue is whether a board could ever become aware of certain actions by the adviser that are violations of law or regulations of the SEC. As noted above and in chapter 2, the recent late-trading and market timing scandals in the mutual fund industry are examples of violations of law or regulations that boards of directors could not have prevented, because they occurred at the adviser level and would never have been brought to the board's attention. That is why no board of directors was ever disciplined for lax oversight in any of these cases. It was obvious that they could not have acted on something they could not have known about.

In this category of improper but undiscoverable activities we would also include such matters as illegally parking assets of the fund with a bank in exchange for favorable treatment in an unrelated transaction, and obtaining additional or indirect compensation by using the assets of a fund for purposes that do not directly benefit the fund. The directors of a fund would not likely be able to discover these violations and thus should not be charged implicitly with responsibility for policing them. However, because information about the adviser's activities flows continuously between the depository bank and the adviser, and because the professional staff of the bank can observe patterns in those activities that might reflect improprieties,

a depository bank would again be more effective in dealing with these conflicts than would a board of directors.

Allocation of Fund Brokerage. How a fund's portfolio transactions are allocated among brokerages poses a special problem, since brokerage fees are the
one area of fund costs that remains with the fund under the Division's UFIC
all-in fee idea. An adviser could obtain benefits for itself, over and above its
all-in fee, by using an affiliated broker or by receiving rebates from brokers for
steering the fund's business to them. To conceal such arrangements, brokers
might rebate to the adviser in the form of securities research or other items or
services of value, rather than cash. Where there is no board to approve the
circumstances under which advisers may use affiliated brokers, the ICA's
prohibition on their use comes into effect. This is not the end of the matter,
however, since advisers can still gain benefits by allocating brokerage to non-
affiliated brokers in return for something of value.

One way to address this problem would be for the investment adviser
to include brokerage costs in the all-in fee. This could be an element of
service that advisers might use to differentiate themselves from others:
investors might regard a higher advisory fee as worth paying in exchange
for relief from the costs of brokerage. The decision to include or not to
include brokerage fees might also vary from fund to fund depending on
how much trading the adviser or the investor expects to be carried on in
managing the portfolio. (In this connection, equity funds would be quite
different from bond funds, which typically engage in far less trading.) In
any event, including brokerage fees in the all-in fee would solve the problem of additional investment adviser compensation through soft dollars.

Even if brokerage were not included in the all-in fee, this is another area
where the depository bank's professional staff would likely provide more
effective oversight than a board. Since the bank would be continuously
accepting and delivering securities on behalf of the fund, and would be in
a position to see the brokerage fees the adviser is paying, the bank's staff
should be able to enforce whatever policies the adviser states in its offering
documents about soft dollar compensation. All brokerage services are not
the same, and advisers should be able to use brokers who, in the adviser's
judgment, will get the best execution for the fund. Accordingly, it is very
difficult for a board of directors to know whether the adviser is using

full-service rather than discount brokers (say) because the services are better or because the adviser is receiving some form of compensation on the side. The bank's professional staff should be able to do this far more easily than a board of independent directors.

Remaining Potential Conflicts. The above discussion indicates that all the statutory or regulatory obligations of a board, as well as many obligations that a board routinely performs under current law, can be accomplished equally well—and in most cases better—by a depository bank functioning as a trustee for investors in the fund. The remaining potential conflicts, which under current law require consultation and approval by the board of directors, or the independent directors alone, include:

- transactions on behalf of the fund with affiliates of the adviser;

- mergers of two or more funds in the same family;

- the possibility that the adviser, in order to achieve better performance, will take greater risks than described in the fund's offering materials; and

- the allocation of scarce securities among different funds managed by the same adviser.

Although each of these problems should be addressed in some way, the creation of a corporate form with a board of directors seems an excessively costly way of doing it. Other alternatives are discussed below.

Current ICA Prohibitions Relating to Transactions with Affiliates. The ICA addresses some obvious conflicts simply by prohibiting certain transactions. Thus section 17 of the act prohibits the sale of securities to or their purchase from an affiliate. The SEC has permitted an exemption from this restriction under certain circumstances, if approved by the fund's independent directors. The purpose of board review in these cases is to ensure that the fund is being fairly treated. The same judgment can certainly be made by the depository bank in its role as trustee. Banks routinely make business judgments of this kind when they serve as trustees for clients—

indeed, bank trustees, as executors of wills and trustees under testamentary trusts, are occasionally given broad authority to make business decisions that might otherwise have been made by a testator, and to decide personal and family matters. There is no reason why the depository bank could not review the facts in these cases and make a decision as to what would be in the best interest of the trust beneficiaries.

Notice Relating to Mergers between Two or More Funds in the Same Complex. Merger transactions occur regularly among business entities. After disclosure of the terms of a proposed merger of corporations, the shareholders of the constituent companies vote to approve or disapprove. Since the proposed MIT would be a trust without a board of directors, there would be no opportunity for the investors to approve such a transaction, and no mechanism through which such approval might occur.

However, one important characteristic of the proposed MIT structure would be substantial ease of exit for investors. Thus investors, having received a description of the proposed merger, would be free to "vote with their feet" by redeeming their shares and taking their money elsewhere. This is a much more significant right for the MIT investor than for the ordinary corporate investor, since the MIT, like an open-end mutual fund, stands ready at all times to redeem shares at their NAV. Hence the investor would suffer no loss of value as a result of the merger announcement itself, and the large number of competing funds means that departing investors can usually find another fund, with an identical investment strategy and similar if not identical costs, relatively quickly. Thus all that seems necessary to assure investors of an opportunity to express their views on a proposed merger is to give them adequate notice.

The same approach could be used in the case of the adviser's sale or assignment of the advisory contract. The adviser would be required to give the investors in the fund adequate notice of the intention to assign, and information about the potential assignee. Dissatisfied investors would then have the opportunity to redeem their shares and take their investments elsewhere.

Dealing with Excessive Risk-taking by the Adviser. Fund advisers are continually tempted to raise the risk profile of the fund portfolio in the pursuit of higher returns, and provisions specifying limits to the fund's risk taking are routinely written into fund offering materials precisely to prevent such overreaching. It is highly unlikely, however, that boards of directors are able to assess whether the adviser is taking greater investment risks than promised either explicitly or implicitly. There are various standard measures of risk, but their application depends crucially on the makeup of each portfolio. Boards that meet only a couple of days each quarter or bimonthly cannot hope to do the thorough analysis required to evaluate risk in each of the portfolios managed by a relatively large fund group. Accordingly, unless the board, at substantial expense, hires specialized consultants for this purpose, assigning this responsibility to the board simply sets it up for failure. In contrast, the depository bank is likely to have on its staff employees who are familiar with the many measures of risk taking that can be used in such an assessment. Here too, then, the depository bank would be a far better monitor of this potential conflict of interest than an independent board.

Allocating Scarce Securities among Different Funds. For a variety of reasons, perhaps because it wants to encourage the development of a liquid market, the underwriter of an initial public offering of securities may not want to place a large portion of the offering in the hands of a mutual fund or MIT that will not be actively trading the securities. For this reason underwriters often set a limit on the number of shares a single investment adviser may purchase. A possible conflict of interest then arises if the adviser manages more than one fund with differing all-in fees. The adviser might have an incentive to place the shares in the fund with the highest fee, since, indirectly, the addition of these shares could result in greater growth for the fund than the shares they replace, and this would raise the adviser's compensation by more than if the shares were allotted to a fund with a lower all-in fee.

Under existing law, the question of how such securities should be allocated is referred to the board of directors. This raises some interesting questions, since the directors have fiduciary obligations to each of their funds separately, and how they resolve conflicts among the funds would be interesting to observe. However, it is doubtful that the issue ever arises in the real world, since the question of whether a security is actually "scarce" is a question of judgment for the adviser. Moreover, even if the security is scarce at the initial public offering (IPO) price, it can probably be purchased in the secondary market at a premium, so the question becomes which fund should receive the shares without the premium. A similar situation arises when an adviser is seeking to acquire a large quantity of securities for more than one of the funds that it manages. The adviser will usually spread out the purchase over time, with the result that the shares are purchased at different prices, and the question again becomes how to allocate the differently priced shares.

From our discussions with industry participants, it appears that advisers are regularly confronted with this issue. The policies that advisers will use in making such allocations among funds are approved in advance by the board of directors and filed with their Form ADV. These policies generally allow advisers to set an average price for all the shares purchased and charge all the funds to which the shares are allocated that average price. Other arrangements are detailed for sales and other contingencies. In any event, filing policies and seeing that those policies are followed should be sufficient for addressing this potential conflict. The SEC, in its regular examinations, could review compliance with this policy, or the depository bank could do so.

Accordingly, while there are numerous "conflict of interest" issues that are routinely handled by boards of directors—as required by the ICA or SEC regulations, or naturally fall to the board as an independent check on the adviser—they can all be addressed effectively, and in some cases more effectively, by the professional staff of a trustee bank.

Reducing the Obstacles to Moving from Fund to Fund

A key element of any competitive market is the ability of customers to move freely from one competitor to another in search of the best value for their money. In general, mutual fund investors face little friction in switching between funds, but to ensure that competition grows as intended following the introduction of MITs (or any similar reform), policymakers should consider concomitant changes in the ICA and in the tax laws to make moving an investment from one fund to another as easy as possible.

In general, two principal obstacles, taxes and front- and back-end loads, create most of the limitations on an investor's movement of funds. In the discussion that follows we offer some ideas that address both issues.

Tax Changes. The current system of taxation for mutual funds originated in the Revenue Act of 1936. The central component of this legislation was a surtax imposed on undistributed corporate profits, a measure intended to collect taxes from individuals who, to avoid taxes on dividends, were shifting their investments to firms with lower levels of distribution.[10] However, because mutual funds are meant for collective investment and not to be run as a "normal business corporation,"[11] Congress gave them a special designation under which they pay corporate taxes only on profits not distributed to shareholders—income distributed to shareholders is passed through to them untaxed. This provision continues today under Subchapter M of the Internal Revenue Code of 1986.

To retain its status as a regulated investment company and avoid taxes on distributions, a mutual fund must distribute to shareholders at least 90 percent of earnings in any fiscal year. Moreover, a mutual fund "must distribute 98 percent of its net realized gains over a twelve-month period ending October 31 and net investment income every calendar year ending in December." The fund pays the corporate tax rate on any remaining undistributed income or realized capital gains, as well as a 4 percent excise tax on the difference between the required 98 percent distribution and the amount actually distributed.[12]

Because mutual funds, in compliance with this law, pass through essentially all their profits, their investors receive distributions annually—and incur the accompanying capital gains taxes—for doing nothing more than holding their shares. (Of total mutual fund assets in 2005, roughly half incurred taxes on distributions; another 7 percent of total assets were held in funds invested in tax-exempt securities, and 47 percent in tax-deferred funds such as 401(k) plans and IRAs.[13]) In addition, of course, when investors redeem shares at their NAV, they pay a capital gains tax on the difference between the cost basis of the shares and their value on the date of redemption.

This has led many industry observers to assail the tax scheme as inefficient and unfair in several respects. First, although a fund has to pass through all its profits to investors, it cannot "pass through" its losses; rather, the fund may offset its own capital gains and carry excess losses forward for future use for up to eight years. This arrangement prevents shareholders—who can deduct up to $3,000 in capital losses each year—from managing losses in the way that is best for them.[14]

Second, the distribution of profits complicates the investor's decisions about when to purchase shares. The problem with current-year distributions is that the shareholder on the distribution date pays tax on a pro rata share of all income and gains recognized up to that date, whether that shareholder owned the mutual fund for a day, a year, or a decade, and without regard to when the gain accrued. For tax purposes these distributions are treated as a return *on* capital, even though at the fund level an adjustment is made to the per-share NAV as if the fund shareholder received a return *of* capital. As an example of this phenomenon (which is often called "buying the dividend"), consider a case where a fund distributed 10 percent of the NAV as dividends and capital gains the day after a new investor purchased shares in the fund. The new investor would be taxed on 10 percent of the new investment, even though he or she was not a shareholder (and received no appreciation) when these gains accrued to the fund, and even though the fund's NAV fell by the 10 percent distribution on the day it was made.[15]

Third, a related complication is the issue of "tax overhang," which occurs when a fund owns securities that have appreciated considerably. If the fund ends up selling some of them, new investors will incur taxes on distributions even though they did not benefit from the appreciation themselves.[16]

Over the long term, the system of forced distributions by mutual funds can wreak havoc on returns. According to Lipper, in 2005 alone investors paid at least $6.3 billion in taxes on long-term capital gains distributions "for doing nothing more than buying and holding their funds." The study asks, "Can you imagine the power of compounding these amounts over long periods?"[17] In fact, had it not been for the 2003 tax cuts that lowered rates on capital gains and dividend income to 15 percent, the tax liability would have been considerably higher. Consequently, for the past several years, legislation has been introduced in Congress that would defer taxes on mutual fund capital gains passed through to shareholders. Most recently, in January 2007, Rep. Jim Saxton (R-NJ) introduced H.R. 397, which would exempt capital gains from taxation provided they are automatically reinvested in additional shares of the fund.[18]

Congress as a whole had acted previously on this issue with the Mutual Fund Tax Awareness Act of 2000, which "instructed the SEC to require improved disclosure of after-tax returns for mutual funds." The SEC then followed with its 2001 rule requiring funds to disclose standardized after-tax returns for one-, five-, and ten-year periods.[19]

What matters for this discussion is that current tax policies have an adverse impact on the willingness or ability of investors to move from fund to fund. An investor switching from fund A to fund B might have to pay capital gains tax not only on the shares redeemed from fund A, but also on previously accumulated capital gains in the fund B shares being purchased. To remove these obstacles to the movement of investors among collective investment media, including the proposed MIT, we recommend an overhaul of tax rules in this area. At a minimum, investors should be able to carry over their tax basis in mutual fund shares, or their MIT equivalent, if within a short time after redeeming those shares or units they reinvest the proceeds in another collective investment vehicle. This one change would remove a significant tax-related obstacle to competition among funds and their advisers.

Loads. Front-end and back-end loads also impair the ability of investors to move from fund to fund and hence reduce competition among mutual funds and advisers. Because so much of the distribution process is moving toward financial and other advisers, who are compensated through 12b-1 fees, inclusion of 12b-1 fees or their equivalent in the adviser's all-in fee will solve much of the problem. Beyond that, front- and back-end fees should be refunded or waived if, within a limited period—say, six months—after an investor buys shares in a mutual fund or MIT, a major event occurs that changes the character of the fund. Such triggering events might include a substantial increase in the adviser's all-in fee, a merger of the fund with another, or a change in advisers.

What the MIT Option Will Do

As the SEC's Division of Investment Management did with its original UFIC proposal, we offer the MIT not as a substitute for the existing mutual fund system but as an additional, optional way to organize collective investment. We do this for two reasons. First, many investors are quite satisfied with the current system, both the way it works and the returns they receive. They include many who may feel comfortable—certainly at the beginning—in keeping their funds in the corporate structure that has existed for over sixty-five years. We see no reason to force these investors to change.

However, it is also our view that introducing the MIT idea as an alternative, competing system is in keeping with our emphasis and reliance on competition. If we are correct that the MIT structure will stimulate competition among investment advisers and produce lower costs for investors, it will supplant the existing system over time. In any event, if competition develops among MITs, as we think it will, the effect will be to drive down costs along the entire collective investment spectrum, including conventional mutual funds.

Ultimately, of course, the marketplace will determine the outcome. In essence, in recommending the MIT structure, we are advocating price deregulation in the mutual fund industry, by at least offering the option of eliminating boards of directors as price regulators. In other settings in the U.S. economy, where policymakers have deregulated prices in industries that are structurally competitive, there is clear evidence that deregulation has resulted in substantial savings to consumers.[20] The same should occur with mutual funds. Indeed, the improvement of investment conditions for consumers—encouraging lower prices, greater efficiency, and more innovation—was the motivation for this study, just as it should be the objective of policymakers.

Notes

Chapter 1: A New Look at Mutual Funds

1. William J. Baumol and others, *The Economics of Mutual Fund Markets: Competition Versus Regulation* (Boston: Kluwer Academic Publishers, 1990), 27.

2. To be sure, different index funds track the underlying index in different ways, using different baskets of securities that closely approximate the value of the index. These differences in tracking account for the minor differences in the performance of funds tracking the same index and can account for differences in the composition of index funds over time.

3. John C. Bogle, *The Battle for the Soul of Capitalism* (New Haven: Yale University Press, 2005), 162.

4. See, for example, Paul A. Samuelson and William D. Nordhaus, *Economics*, 18th ed. (New York: McGraw-Hill Irwin, 2005), 149–50: "Total profit reaches its peak—is maximized—when there is no longer any extra profit to be earned by selling extra output. At the maximum-profit point, the last unit produced brings in an amount of revenue exactly equal to that unit's cost. What is that extra revenue? It is the price per unit. What is that extra cost? It is the marginal cost. . . . A profit-maximizing firm will set its output at that level where marginal cost equals price." See also Karl E. Case and Ray C. Fair, *Principles of Economics*, 2nd ed. (Englewood Cliffs, NJ: Prentice-Hall, 1992), 235–36.

5. Friedrich A. Hayek, "Competition as a Discovery Procedure," in *New Studies in Philosophy, Politics, Economics and the History of Ideas* (London: Routledge & Kegan Paul, 1982), 179–90.

6. Tom Lauricella, "Independent Directors Strike Back," *Wall Street Journal*, July 5, 2006.

7. John C. Coates IV and R. Glenn Hubbard, "Competition and Shareholder Fees in the Mutual Fund Industry: Evidence and Implications for Policy" (Working Paper 127, American Enterprise Institute, June 2006), www.aei.org/publication24577 (accessed January 16, 2007).

8. The wide dispersion in fees occurs even with S&P 500 index funds, in which the products being offered essentially have the same investment objective, management style, and risk-return profile. According to one study, "despite the financial homogeneity of S&P 500 index funds, this sector exhibits the fund proliferation and

fee dispersion observed in the broader industry." Ali Hortaçsu and Chad Syverson, "Product Differentiation, Search Costs, and Competition in the Mutual Fund Industry: A Case Study of S&P 500 Index Funds," *Quarterly Journal of Economics* 119 (May, 2004): 403. They argue that the dispersion is due, at least in part, to investors valuing nonfinancial fund differentiation (in areas such as fund age, total number of funds in the fund family, and tax exposure) and to the fact that novice investors with high information and search costs have purchased shares of higher-price funds.

9. For example, see James J. Choi, David Laibson, and Brigitte C. Madrian, "Why Does the Law of One Price Fail? An Experiment on Index Mutual Funds" (Working Paper 12261, National Bureau of Economic Research, Cambridge, MA, May 2006), papers.nber.org/papers/w12261 (accessed December 12, 2006). The authors argue that the problem is insufficient disclosure.

10. Lipper, "A Comparison of Mutual Fund Expenses Across the Atlantic," Lipper Fund*Industry* Insight Reports, September 2005, 5, 10.

11. General Accounting Office (now known as the Government Accountability Office) (GAO), *Mutual Fund Fees: Additional Disclosure Could Encourage Price Competition* (June 2000), 56, www.gao.gov/archive/2000/gg00126.pdf (accessed December 18, 2006).

12. U.S. Securities and Exchange Commission (SEC), *Investment Trusts and Investment Companies, Report of the Securities and Exchange Commission* (Washington, DC: U.S. Government Printing Office, 1939–40).

13. U.S. SEC, Division of Investment Management, *Protecting Investors: A Half Century of Investment Company Regulation* (Washington, DC: U.S. Government Printing Office, 1992), 267, note 64.

14. Ibid., 255–56.

15. Ibid., 256.

16. Senate Committee on Banking and Currency, *Investment Company Amendments Act of 1969*, 91st Cong., 1st sess., 1969, S. Rep. 184, 5.

17. John P. Freeman and Stewart L. Brown, "Mutual Fund Advisory Fees: The Cost of Conflicts of Interest," *Journal of Corporation Law* 26 (Spring 2001): 613.

18. The idea that a collective investment structure could be contractual, rather than through a corporation, was outlined by Paula Tkac, an economist at the Federal Reserve Bank of Atlanta, at an AEI conference on April 14, 2006. See also, Paula A. Tkac, "Mutual Funds: Temporary Problem or Permanent Morass?" *Economic Review* 89 (Fourth Quarter 2004): 1–21.

19. For example, see Choi, Laibson, and Madrian, "Why Does the Law of One Price Fail?"

Chapter 2: A Brief History of Mutual Fund Regulation

1. Ronald H. Coase, "The Nature of the Firm," *Economica* 4 (November 1937): 386–405.

2. U.S. Securities and Exchange Commission (SEC), Division of Investment Management, *Protecting Investors: A Half Century of Investment Company Regulation* (Washington, DC: U.S. Government Printing Office, 1992), 252.

3. Michael Sevi provided indispensable background research for the discussion of the events that preceded the enactment of the ICA. Michael Sevi, "The Origins and Goals of the Investment Company Act of 1940," AEI, personal memorandum.

4. Thomas P. Lemke, Gerald T. Lins, and A. Thomas Smith III, *Regulation of Investment Companies* (New York: Matthew Bender & Co., 1995), Sec. 2.02.

5. These were the findings of the Senate report on the Investment Company Act of 1940. Senate Committee on Banking and Currency, *Investment Company Act of 1940 and Investment Advisers Act of 1940*, 76th Cong., 3d sess., 1940, S. Rep. 1775, 3.

6. Ibid., 2.

7. U.S. SEC, *Investment Trusts and Investment Companies, Report of the Securities and Exchange Commission*, Part III (Washington, D.C.: U.S. Government Printing Office, 1940), 804.

8. Ibid.

9. Ibid.

10. Ibid.

11. Ibid., 805.

12. Senate Committee on Banking and Currency, *Investment Company Act of 1940 and Investment Advisers Act of 1940*, 4.

13. "The Investment Company Act of 1940," *Yale Law Journal* 50 (January 1941): 442–43.

14. One study estimated that "the average fund managed by an investigated firm lost approximately $14.0 million in assets over the 6-month window after the announcement" of the SEC, New York Attorney General, or other regulatory body. Since the investigated firms managed 4,250 funds and fund share classes between September 2003 and June 2004, aggregate losses in assets totaled approximately $60 billion. See Todd Houge and Jay Wellman, "Fallout from the Mutual Fund Trading Scandal," *Journal of Business Ethics* 62 (2005): 129–39, www.biz.uiowa.edu/faculty/thouge/fund_scandal_JBE.pdf (accessed January 9, 2007).

15. Investment Company Institute (ICI), *2006 Investment Company Fact Book* (Washington, D.C., Investment Company Institute, 2006), 18.

16. ICI, "Fees and Expenses of Mutual Funds, 2005," *Fundamentals* 15 (June 2006): 4, www.icinet.net/pdf/fm-v15n4.pdf (accessed December 19, 2006).

17. Wharton School of Finance and Commerce, *A Study of Mutual Funds*, 87th Cong., 2nd sess., 1962, H. Rep. 2274; U.S. SEC, *Public Policy Implications of Investment Company Growth*, 89th Cong., 2nd sess., 1966, H. Rep. 2337. For a useful, concise summary of the history of the 1940 acts and subsequent refinements through the late 1980s, see William J. Baumol and others, *The Economics of Mutual Fund Markets: Competition Versus Regulation* (Boston: Kluwer Academic Publishers, 1990).

18. Martin E. Lybecker, "Enhanced Corporate Governance for Mutual Funds: A Flawed Concept that Deserves Serious Reconsideration," *Washington University Law Quarterly* 83 (2005): 1054–55.

19. Ibid., 1055–56.

20. U.S. SEC, Division of Investment Management, *Protecting Investors: A Half Century of Investment Company Regulation* (Washington, DC: U.S. Government Printing Ofiice, 1992), 267.

21. Larry D. Barnett, "When Is a Mutual Fund Director Independent? The Unexplored Role of Professional Relationships Under Section 2(a)(19) of the Investment Company Act," *DePaul Business and Commercial Law Journal* 4 (Winter 2006): 164. Also see U.S. Securities and Exchange Commission, "Role of Independent Directors of Investment Companies," Investment Company Act Release 24816, *Federal Register* 66 (10): 3734 (January 16, 2001).

22. U.S. SEC, "Role of Independent Directors," 3736.

23. U.S. SEC, "Investment Company Governance," Investment Company Act Release 26520, *Federal Register* 69 (147): 46378 (August 2, 2004).

24. See Peter J. Wallison, "Landmark Ruling," *AEI Financial Services Outlook*, May 2006, www.aei.org/publication24303 (accessed October 12, 2006).

25. U.S. SEC, Investment Company Act Release 12888 (December 10, 1982). Available through Westlaw (1982 WL 523380).

26. See Baumol and others, *The Economics of Mutual Fund Markets*, 61–63.

27. The SEC later argued that late-trading violates rules 22c-1, also known as the "forward pricing rule," issued in 1968 under the Investment Company Act of 1940 specifically to prevent this kind of activity.

28. The term is also used in a different sense, to mean trying to guess a peak or trough in a market index and buy or sell accordingly.

29. The New York State attorney general used the same provision in the Martin Act to prosecute cases against investment banks and their analysts for publicly recommending the purchases of stocks whose prospects they were privately skeptical about (or worse).

30. The New York State attorney general lost the only late-trading case that actually went to trial, a case brought against a broker who facilitated the trades. The jury acquitted the broker on one count and could not reach a verdict on the other four. After the attorney general threatened to retry the broker on those counts, the broker settled, agreeing to a fine and a five-year ban from the securities industry.

31. Tom Lauricella, Monica Langley, and Susan Pulliam, "Spitzer Gambit May Alter Fund-Fee Debate," *Wall Street Journal*, December 11, 2003.

32. Paul Roye, director of the SEC's Division of Investment Management, said in a speech before the Mutual Fund Directors Forum, "In most of the enforcement cases arising out of the scandal, we cannot blame fund boards for the compliance lapses within the funds. Fund managers actually concealed these compliance issues from the board. But troubling questions persist as to why management personnel were able to

successfully conceal these problems. What questions could have been asked that would have unraveled the frauds at an early stage? What steps could boards have taken that would have prevented the types of abuses we are seeing?" Paul F. Roye, " Critical Issues for Investment Company Directors," remarks before the Mutual Fund Directors Forum, Fifth Annual Policy Conference (Washington, D.C., February 17, 2005), www.sec.gov/news/speech/spch021705pfr.htm (accessed January 11, 2007).

Chapter 3: The Growth of the Mutual Fund Industry and Its Competitors

1. Federal Deposit Insurance Corporation (FDIC), *Statistics on Depository Institutions*, www2.fdic.gov/SDI/main.asp (accessed December 14, 2006).

2. T. Neil Bathon, presentation at the AEI conference, "Competition for Mutual Funds from New Collective Investment Vehicles," Washington, D.C., April 26, 2006 (transcript available at www.aei.org/event1312).

3. Investment Company Institute and Securities Industry Association, "Equity Ownership in America: 2005," www.sia.com/research/pdf/EquityOwnership05.pdf (accessed June 28, 2006).

4. Assets of closed-end funds also continued to grow during the postwar period, but at a much slower pace than those of open-end funds. In particular, between 1995 and 2002, total assets held in closed-end funds hovered around $150 billion, but by year-end 2005 they had almost doubled, to $276 billion (of which bond funds accounted for about $172 billion and equity funds about $105 billion). See Investment Company Institute (ICI), *2006 Investment Company Fact Book* (Washington, D.C.: Investment Company Institute, 2006), 32–36.

5. For example, Robert Shiller has calculated the real (inflation-adjusted) annual return to stocks over 1950–2004 to have been 7.6 percent. Taking into account inflation, this would put the nominal annual return in the 10 percent range. See Robert J. Shiller, "The Life-Cycle Personal Accounts Proposal for Social Security: An Evaluation" (Working Paper 11300, National Bureau of Economic Research, Cambridge, MA), April 2005, www.nber.org/papers/w11300 (accessed December 14, 2006). Jeremy Siegel has calculated a slightly higher annual nominal return on stocks of 11.2 percent, based on the performance of the S&P 500 index, over the 1957–2003 period. Use of this rate of return would not materially change the calculations in the text. See Jeremy J. Siegel, *The Future for Investors: Why the Tried and the True Triumph over the Bold and the New* (New York: Crown Business, 2005), 42.

6. The nature and magnitude of the tax incentives for both plans have been revised and expanded since by Congress several times. A counterpart of the 401(k) plan exists for nonprofit institutions, called the 403(b) plan.

7. See Burton G. Malkiel, *A Random Walk Down Wall Street*, 6th ed. (New York: W. W. Norton & Company, 1996).

8. ICI, *2006 Investment Company Fact Book*, 67.

9. Ibid., 47.

10. ICI, "U.S. Household Ownership of Mutual Funds in 2005," *Fundamentals* 14 (October 2005): 6, www.ici.org/pdf/fm-v14n5.pdf (accessed December 14, 2006).

11. U.S. General Accounting Office (now known as the Government Accountability Office) (GAO), *Mutual Fund Fees: Additional Disclosure Could Encourage Price Competition* (June 2000), 56, www.gao.gov/archive/2000/gg00126.pdf (accessed December 18, 2006).

12. ICI, *2006 Investment Company Fact Book*, 13–14.

13. Ibid., 50.

14. Ibid., 9.

15. Ibid., 44.

16. Because they are partly customized, SMAs are generally more expensive than mutual funds, although "[a]t the high end, separate accounts are price competitive, and often cheaper, than mutual fund portfolios." See Sam White and Todd Smurl, "Get Your Adviser to Open Up," Forbes.com, December 27, 2006, www.forbes.com/investoreducation/2006/12/27/open-architecture-smartleaf-pf-invedu-in_sw_1227soapbox_inl.html (accessed January 12, 2007). In fact, as mentioned in chapter 4, data from Morningstar show substantial convergence in the fees charged by money managers to the registered representatives who market SMAs to clients, which suggests that competition is a major factor in determining the pricing for this collective investment product.

17. Money Management Institute, "SMA Assets Reach Record $805.8 Billion in 3Q 2006," www.moneyinstitute.com/downloads/2006/12/3q06pressrelease.pdf (accessed January 12, 2007).

18. Money Management Institute, "Second Quarter Data," www.moneyinstitute.com/downloads/2006/09/2q06numbers.pdf (accessed January 12, 2007).

19. American Bankers Association, "2004 Analysis of Trust Fund Performance."

20. Diya Gullapalli, "SEC to Hasten Process to Clear ETF Approvals," *Wall Street Journal*, December 11, 2006.

21. Bathon, presentation at Competition for Mutual Funds from New Collective Investment Vehicles conference.

22. See U.S. Securities and Exchange Commission (SEC), "Actively Managed Exchange-Traded Funds," Investment Company Act Release 25258 (November 8, 2001), www.sec.gov/rules/concept/ic-25258.htm (accessed January 9, 2007).

23. See U.S. SEC, "Prohibition of Fraud by Advisers to Certain Pooled Investment Vehicles; Accredited Investors in Certain Private Investment Vehicles," Investment Advisers Act Release 2576 (December 27, 2006), www.sec.gov/rules/proposed/2006/33-8766.pdf (accessed January 9, 2007).

24. See President's Working Group on Financial Markets, *Hedge Funds, Leverage, and the Lessons of Long-Term Capital Management*, April 1999. http://www.ustreas.gov/pressreleases/reports/hedgfund.pdf (accessed February 14, 2007): Appendix B, B1–B4.

25. Bathon, presentation at Competition for Mutual Funds from New Collective Investment Vehicles conference.

Chapter 4: The Paradox of Mutual Fund Fees

1. See John C. Bogle, *The Battle for the Soul of Capitalism* (New Haven, CT: Yale University Press, 2005).

2. See David F. Swensen, *Unconventional Success: A Fundamental Approach to Personal Investment* (New York: Free Press, 2005).

3. General Accounting Office (now known as the Government Accountability Office) (GAO), *Mutual Fund Fees: Additional Disclosure Could Encourage Price Competition* (June 2000), 56, www.gao.gov/archive/2000/gg00126.pdf (accessed December 18, 2006).

4. John P. Freeman and Stewart L. Brown, "Mutual Fund Advisory Fees: The Cost of Conflicts of Interest," *Journal of Corporation Law* 26 (Spring 2001): 655.

5. See John C. Coates IV and R. Glenn Hubbard, "Competition and Shareholder Fees in the Mutual Fund Industry: Evidence and Implications for Policy" (Working Paper 127, American Enterprise Institute, June 2006), www.aei.org/publication24577 (accessed January 12, 2007).

6. William J. Baumol and others, *The Economics of Mutual Fund Markets: Competition Versus Regulation* (Boston: Kluwer Academic Publishers, 1990).

7. See also Ali Hortaçsu and Chad Syverson, "Product Differentiation, Search Costs, and Competition in the Mutual Fund Industry: A Case Study of S&P 500 Index Funds," *Quarterly Journal of Economics* 119 (May 2004): 403–56.

8. Figures 4-1, 4-2, and 4-3 show that although the dispersion of expense ratios among U.S. funds is greater than that of U.K. funds, expense ratios in the United States are lower on average. This is probably attributable to greater economies of scale among U.S. funds. The Lipper report suggests that this is the case and contains another table showing that the average fund size in the sample of U.S. funds used for this study was $3.2 billion, almost five times as large as the average U.K. fund, at $688 million. Lipper, "A Comparison of Mutual Fund Expenses Across the Atlantic," Lipper Fund*Industry* Insight Reports, September 2005, 5, 10.

9. We prepared this description of the organization of separately managed accounts with the help of Steve Deutsch of Morningstar (personal correspondence).

10. This is not to say that price competition does not exist in the mutual fund industry, but only that it is not the vigorous competition normally displayed by industries with many competitors, ease of entry, and relative ease of consumer switching. Indeed, one study found that high-cost fund families could increase their market share by lowering their prices, but low-cost fund families could *increase* their fees without losing market share. See Ajay Khorana and Henri Servaes, "Conflicts of Interest and Competition in the Mutual Fund Industry" (July 2004), 3–4, downloadable at ssrn.com/abstract=240596 (accessed December 20, 2006).

11. U.S. Securities and Exchange Commission (SEC), Division of Investment Management, *Protecting Investors: A Half-Century of Investment Company Regulation* (Washington, DC: U.S. Government Printing Office, 1992), 256.

12. U.S. SEC, *Public Policy Implications of Investment Company Growth*, 148. This notion has persisted. In its 1992 report the SEC's Division of Investment Management summarized the views of industry critics as follows: "Critics of the role assigned by the Act to investment company directors, and particularly the independent directors, believe that because an investment company is a creature of its sponsor/adviser, it is difficult for directors to provide effective oversight. Because an investment company usually is managed by its sponsor or an affiliate, they argue, the independent directors are not truly independent, and have little choice but to approve the fee levels that the adviser deems necessary to operate the company and market its shares... These critics also point out that independent directors almost never fire the adviser, and while they sometimes negotiate a fee rate below that proposed by the adviser, the amount of the reduction is usually marginal." U.S. SEC, Division of Investment Management, *Protecting Investors*, 264.

13. In 2003, John Montgomery, founder and president of Bridgeway Funds, argued, "Why not make the board put the management contract up for bid if the current adviser shows repeated underperformance? For example, if the adviser is in the bottom quartile for five of six years, or if the adviser is in the bottom quartile for three of four years and has a net expense ratio in the bottom 10%, mandate that the contract is opened to competitive bids. This type of requirement combined with the disclosure I just mentioned would do much to make the board more accountable to the shareholders." See John Montgomery, statement before the House Financial Services Committee Subcommittee on Capital Markets, Insurance and Government Sponsored Enterprises, Hearing "Mutual Fund Industry Practices and their Effect on Individual Investors," March 12, 2003, 108th Cong., 1st Sess. (available through LexisNexis).

14. See *Chamber of Commerce of the United States v. SEC*, 412 F.3d 133 (DC Cir. 2005) and *Chamber of Commerce of the United States v. SEC*, 443 F.3d 890 (DC Cir. 2006). In two separate opinions, the court ruled that the SEC had violated the Administrative Procedure Act by failing to consider the effect that its regulation would have on the promotion of efficiency, competition, and capital formation—three requirements placed in the ICA by the National Securities Markets Improvement Act of 1996.

15. U.S. SEC, Division of Investment Management, *Report on Mutual Fund Fees and Expenses*, December 2000, www.sec.gov/news/studies/feestudy.htm (accessed December 20, 2006).

16. Investment Company Institute (ICI), *2006 Investment Company Fact Book* (Washington, D.C.: 2006), 46.

17. The survey was conducted December 14–19, 2005, with a minimum of 1,000 interviews. The margin of error was plus or minus 3.09 percent. The full survey report is available from AEI.

18. U.S. SEC, "Consolidated Disclosure of Mutual Fund Expenses," Investment Company Act Release 16244 (February 1, 1988); see also U.S. SEC, "Shareholder Reports and Quarterly Portfolio Disclosure of Registered Management Investment Companies," Investment Company Act Release 26372 (February 27, 2004), *Federal Register* 69 (46): 11244–73.

19. U.S. SEC, "Shareholder Reports and Quarterly Portfolio Disclosure," 11245 (March 9, 2004).

20. U.S. SEC, "Confirmation Requirements and Point of Sale Disclosure Requirements for Transactions in Certain Mutual Funds and Other Securities, and Other Confirmation Requirement Amendments, and Amendments to the Registration Form for Mutual Funds," Investment Company Act Release 26341 (January 29, 2004), *Federal Register* 69 (27): 6438–98. This proposal was republished in March 2005 to obtain further public comments. See U.S. SEC, "Point of Sale Disclosure Requirements and Confirmation Requirements for Transactions in Mutual Funds, College Savings Plans, and Certain Other Securities, and Amendments to the Registration Form for Mutual Funds," Investment Company Act Release 26778, (February 28, 2005), *Federal Register* 70 (42): 10521–57.

21. ICI, "Understanding Investor Preferences for Mutual Fund Information: Summary of Research Findings," 2006, www.ici.org/pdf/rpt_06_inv_prefs_summary.pdf (accessed December 20, 2006).

22. For example, see Bogle, *The Battle for the Soul of Capitalism*, 161.

23. For example, Bogle points out (*The Battle for the Soul of Capitalism*, 158–59) the well-known lag in the annual return of the average actively managed mutual fund behind the market as a whole—during 1985–2004 the difference was 2.8 percentage points—as measured by the annual return on the S&P 500 index. He attributes this entire difference to unnecessary mutual fund fees. But one can also characterize the difference in returns as simply reflecting the fact that mutual fund managers on average cannot beat the market, as has been frequently demonstrated, perhaps no better than by Princeton's Burton Malkiel in successive editions of his classic *A Random Walk Down Wall Street*. This does not mean that fees on actively managed funds are necessarily excessive or that fund boards necessarily have failed to discipline advisers, but only that the product itself (actively managed funds) does not perform as well as a particular index. Despite this difference in opinion about fees, we do agree with Bogle that fee competition could be improved, but not by the means he and the SEC, among others, suggest (for reasons we elaborate fully in the text).

24. See, for example, ICI and Independent Directors Council, "Overview of Fund Governance Practices, 1994–2004," 2006, www.ici.org/pdf/rpt_fund_gov_practices.pdf (accessed December 20, 2006).

25. The ICI nonetheless points to declines in fund expense ratios over recent years: "Fees and Expenses of Mutual Funds, 2005," *Fundamentals* 15 (June 2006), www.icinet.net/pdf/fm-v15n4.pdf (accessed December 20, 2006). This seems to be true for the largest and most competitive funds, toward which fund investment is

slowly migrating. However, the evidence on this is not clear for all funds, even on an asset-weighted basis, and seems to depend on whether one is measuring average or median expense ratios. A Lipper research study, *Global Themes in the Mutual Fund Industry—2005: A Review of the Global Pooled Investment Management Industry* (February 2006), found that "the asset-weighted average (AWA) total expense ratio (TER) for all open-end funds increased from 0.774% in 2004 to 0.785% in 2005" but that "the median TER declined from 1.279% to 1.256% over the same period" (page 2 of the U.S. survey section).

26. Tom Lauricella, "Independent Directors Strike Back," *Wall Street Journal*, July 5, 2006.

27. Freeman and Brown, "Mutual Fund Advisory Fees," 613.

28. *Gartenberg v. Merrill Lynch Asset Management, Inc.*, 694 F.2d 923 (2nd Cir. 1982).

29. *Gartenberg*, 930.

30. *Gartenberg*, 929.

31. Alfred E. Kahn, *The Economics of Regulation: Principles and Institutions*, vol. 2 (Cambridge, MA: MIT Press, 1988), 48.

32. *Gartenberg*, 929.

33. In fact, in its 2000 report, *Mutual Fund Fees and Expenses*, the SEC staff insisted that "fund directors should . . . attempt to ensure that an appropriate portion of the cost savings from any available economies of scale is passed along to fund shareholders."

34. See Kahn, *The Economics of Regulation*, vol. 1, 63–67.

35. Ibid., 29–30.

36. See Frederick A. Hayek, "Competition as a Discovery Procedure," in *New Studies in Philosophy, Politics, Economics and the History of Ideas* (London: Routledge & Kegan Paul, 1982), 179–90.

37. Roman L. Weil, "Allocations of Cost and Revenue," in *Handbook of Cost Management*, 2nd ed., eds. Roman L. Weil and Michael W. Maher (Hoboken, NJ: John Wiley & Sons, 2005), 467.

38. See, for example, John C. Bogle, *Common Sense on Mutual Funds: New Imperatives for the Intelligent Investor* (New York: John Wiley & Sons, 1999).

39. The story of the conversion from Wellington Management, a corporate adviser to the Wellington Fund, to the mutual structure in which the Wellington Fund became the owner of its investment adviser—later to become Vanguard—is told in detail in Robert Slater, *John Bogle and the Vanguard Experiment: One Man's Quest to Transform the Mutual Fund Industry* (Chicago: Irwin Professional Publishing, 1996).

40. *Gartenberg*, 929.

41. See Karl E. Case and Ray C. Fair, *Principles of Economics*, 2nd ed. (Englewood Cliffs, NJ: Prentice-Hall, 1992), 235–36; Paul A. Samuelson and William D. Nordhaus, *Economics*, 18th ed. (New York: McGraw-Hill Irwin, 2005), 149–50.

42. GAO, "Mutual Fund Fees."

43. ICI, *Understanding Shareholders' Use of Information and Advisers* (Spring 1997), www.ici.org/pdf/rpt_undstnd_share.pdf (accessed December 21, 2006).

44. GAO, *Mutual Fund Fees*, 73.

45. Ibid., 62–64.

46. Ibid., 77.

47. Stephen K. West, *The Investment Company Industry in the 1990's* (report for the Investment Company Institute, Washington, D.C.: ICI, March 1990), 64.

48. Ibid., 65–66.

49. U.S. SEC, Division of Investment Management, *Protecting Investors*, 282.

50. Ibid., 283.

51. Ibid., 332–45. West eventually modified his UIF proposal to bring it closer to the UFIC structure. The principal change was to restructure the UIF as a corporation rather than a contractual relationship with an investment adviser, and to reestablish the board of directors as the source of shareholders' protection against the conflicts of interest of the adviser. West's UFIC approach was outlined at an AEI conference, Is There a Better Way to Regulate Mutual Funds? September 26, 2005. A transcript is available at www.aei.org/event1149 (accessed February 26, 2006).

52. U.S. SEC, Division of Investment Management, *Protecting Investors*, 337.

53. Ibid., 339.

54. Ibid., 340.

55. See, for example, Paul A. London, *The Competition Solution: The Bipartisan Secret behind American Prosperity* (Washington, DC: AEI Press, 2005).

56. U.S. SEC, Division of Investment Management, *Protecting Investors*, 341.

57. Ibid., 341.

58. Ibid., 309.

Chapter 5: The Managed Investment Trust Option

1. Dechert LLP, *Survey of Collective Investment Structures* (Washington, D.C.: Investment Company Institute, December 2005).

2. Soft dollar compensation arises because advisers are able to charge brokerage commissions to the funds they advise, but may receive benefits in return from the brokerage firm that executes the order. The most common benefit is research, which has value to advisers because it may relieve them of employing an analyst to do the same task. But soft dollar compensation can also include more tangible compensation, which can look like a rebate of a portion of the brokerage commission under some circumstances.

3. Investment Management Association, *Review of the Governance Arrangements of United Kingdom Authorised Collective Investment Schemes*, February 2005, 16, www. investmentuk.org/news/research/2005/topic/unit_trusts/cisgovernance.pdf (accessed December 22, 2006).

4. See the remarks of Richard Saunders at the AEI conference, The Regulation and Structure of Collective Investment Vehicles Outside the United States, Washington,

DC, May 18, 2006. Transcript available at www.aei.org/event1318 (accessed February 26, 2007).

5. A recent academic study concluded that boards of directors overseeing large numbers of funds were less effective at preventing scandals, whether or not they had independent chairs: "Overall, our results cast doubt on the usefulness of the new SEC requirements for a supermajority of independent directors and an independent chairman. Contrary to the arguments made in support of these requirements, we find that board and chairman independence are generally insignificant factors in explaining the level of fund fees or the likelihood of a fund scandal. We contend that board size, the number of funds overseen by each independent director, and independent director compensation are significant aspects of fund governance that should receive greater regulatory attention." Stephen P. Ferris and Xuemin (Sterling) Yan, "Do Independent Directors and Chairmen Really Matter? The Role of Boards of Directors in Mutual Fund Governance" (February 2005), downloadable at ssrn.com/abstract= 681526 (accessed December 22, 2006).

6. See, for example, Peter J. Wallison, "Groundhog Day: Reliving Deregulation Debates," *AEI Financial Services Outlook*, October 2006, www.aei.org/publication 25034 (accessed February 12, 2007).

7. These examples are drawn in part from a series of public conferences at AEI between September 2005 and May 2006, particularly the conference on Stephen K. West's UFIC proposal on September 26, 2005, and Paula Tkac's presentation on April 14, 2006. Transcripts of all these conferences are available at www.aei.org/mutual-funds (accessed February 12, 2007). In both cases, independent directors of mutual funds suggested roles for a board in addressing conflicts of interest on the part of the adviser that were separate from the approval of the adviser's fees and expenses.

8. *SEC v. Capital Gains Research Bureau, Inc.*, 375 U.S. 180 (1963), 191–92.

9. U.S. SEC, Division of Investment Management, *Protecting Investors: A Half Century of Investment Company Regulation* (Washington, D.C.: U.S. Government Printing Office, 1992), 254.

10. Joint Economic Committee, "Encouraging Personal Saving and Investment: Changing the Tax Treatment of Unrealized Capital Gains," June 2000, 4–5, www.house.gov/jec/tax/mutual/mutual.pdf (accessed October 10, 2006).

11. Hearings on H.R. 1192 before the Senate Committee on Finance, 94th Cong. 2nd Sess. (1976), 10–11, reprinted in 196-3 C.B. 28-29. Quoted from Consuelo L. Kertz and Paul J. Simko, "Mutual Fund Investing and Tax Uncertainty: The Need for New Disclosures," *Stanford Journal of Law, Business, and Finance* 7 (Autumn 2001): 107–8.

12. Tom Roseen, *Taxes in the Mutual Fund Industry—2006: Assessing the Impact of Taxes on Shareholders' Returns* (New York: Lipper Research Study, April 2006), 7.

13. ICI, *2006 Investment Company Fact Book* (Washington, D.C., 2006), 15.

14. Roseen, 7–8.

15. Kertz and Simko, "Mutual Fund Investing and Tax Uncertainty," 110.

16. Ibid., 111.

17. Lipper, *Taxes in the Mutual Fund Industry—2006*, 13.

18. According to the bill summary, H.R. 397 "[a]mends the Internal Revenue Code to provide that, in the case of an electing individual, no gain (up to a specified amount) shall be recognized on the receipt of a capital gain dividend distributed by a regulated investment company if such capital gain dividend is automatically reinvested in additional shares of the company pursuant to a dividend reinvestment plan." Available at thomas.loc.gov (accessed February 11, 2007).

19. Lipper, *Taxes in the Mutual Fund Industry—2006*, 12.

20. Clifford W. Winston, "Economic Deregulation: Days of Reckoning for Micro-economists," *Journal of Economic Literature* 31 (September 1993): 1263–89.

Bibliography

American Bankers Association. 2004 Analysis of Trust Fund Performance. http://www.aba.com/Solutions/trust_institution_performance.htm, (accessed June 28, 2006).

American Enterprise Institute. *Is There a Better Way to Regulate Mutual Funds?* AEI Conference Series, Washington, DC, 2005–2006. Transcripts available at http://www.aei.org/mutualfunds (accessed January 18, 2007).

Barnett, Larry D. "When Is a Mutual Fund Director Independent? The Unexplored Role of Professional Relationships under Section 2(a)(19) of the Investment Company Act." *DePaul Business and Commercial Law Journal* 4 (Winter 2006): 155–188.

Bathon, T. Neil. 2006. Presentation, AEI conference, "Competition for Mutual Funds from New Collective Investment Vehicles," Washington, DC, April 26, 2006. Transcript available at http://www.aei.org/event1312 (accessed January 18, 2007).

Baumol, William J., Stephen M. Goldfeld, Lilli A. Gordon, and Michael F., Koehn. *The Economics of Mutual Fund Markets: Competition Versus Regulation.* Boston: Kluwer Academic Publishers, 1990.

Bogle, John C. *Common Sense on Mutual Funds: New Imperatives for the Intelligent Investor.* New York: John Wiley & Sons, 1999.

———. *The Battle for the Soul of Capitalism.* New Haven, CT: Yale University Press, 2005.

Case, Karl E., and Ray C. Fair. *Principles of Economics.* 2nd ed. Englewood Cliffs, NJ: Prentice-Hall, Inc., 1992.

Chamber of Commerce of the United States v. SEC. 412 F. 3d 133 (DC Cir. 2005).

Chamber of Commerce of the United States v. SEC. 443 F. 3d 890 (DC Cir. 2006).

Choi, James J., David Laibson, and Brigitte C. Madrian. "Why Does the Law of One Price Fail? An Experiment on Index Mutual Funds." Working Paper 12261, National Bureau of Economic Research, Cambridge, MA, May 2006. http://papers.nber.org/papers/w12261 (accessed December 12, 2006).

Coase, Ronald H. "The Nature of the Firm." *Economica* 4 (November 1937): 386–405.

Coates, John C., IV, and R. Glenn Hubbard. "Competition and Shareholder Fees in the Mutual Fund Industry: Evidence and Implications for Policy." Working Paper 127, American Enterprise Institute, June 2006. http://www.aei.org/publication24577 (accessed December 12, 2006).

Federal Deposit Insurance Corporation. *Statistics on Depository Institutions*, 2006. http://www2.fdic.gov/SDI/main.asp (accessed December 14, 2006).

Ferris, Stephen P., and Xuemin (Sterling) Yan. "Do Independent Directors and Chairmen Really Matter? The Role of Boards of Directors in Mutual Fund Governance," February 2005. http://ssrn.com/abstract=681526 (accessed December 22, 2006).

Freeman, John P., and Stewart L. Brown. "Mutual Fund Advisory Fees: The Cost of Conflicts of Interest." *Journal of Corporation Law* 26 (Spring 2001): 609–673.

Gartenberg v. Merrill Lynch Asset Management, Inc. 694 F.2d 923 (2nd Cir. 1982).

Gullapalli, Diya. "SEC to Hasten Process to Clear ETF Approvals." *Wall Street Journal*, December 11, 2006.

Hayek, Friedrich. A. "Competition as a Discovery Procedure." In *New Studies in Philosophy, Politics, Economics and the History of Ideas, 179–190*. London: Routledge & Kegan Paul, 1982.

Hedge Fund Research, Inc. 2006. *Hedge Fund Industry Report, Year-End 2005*.

Hortaçsu, Ali, and Chad Syverson. "Product Differentiation, Search Costs, and Competition in the Mutual Fund Industry: A Case Study of S&P 500 Index Funds." *Quarterly Journal of Economics* 119 (May 2004): 403–456.

Houge, Todd, and Jay Wellman. "Fallout from the Mutual Fund Trading Scandal." *Journal of Business Ethics* 62 (2005): 129–139. http://www.biz.uiowa.edu/faculty/thouge/fund_scandal_JBE.pdf (accessed January 9, 2007).

"The Investment Company Act of 1940." *Yale Law Journal* 50 (January 1941): 440–457.

Investment Company Institute. *Understanding Shareholders' Use of Information and Advisers*, Spring 1997. http://www.ici.org/pdf/rpt_undstnd_share.pdf (accessed December 21, 2006).

———. "U.S. Household Ownership of Mutual Funds in 2005." *Fundamentals* 14 (October 2005). http://www.ici.org/pdf/fm-v14n5.pdf (accessed December 14, 2006).

———. *Survey of Collective Investment Structures*. Washington, DC: Investment Company Institute, December 2005.

———. *2006 Investment Company Fact Book*. Washington, DC: Investment Company Institute, 2006.

———. "Understanding Investor Preferences for Mutual Fund Information: Summary of Research Findings," 2006. http://www.ici.org/pdf/rpt_06_inv_prefs_summary.pdf (accessed December 20, 2006).

———. "Fees and Expenses of Mutual Funds, 2005." *Fundamentals* 15 (June 2006). http://www.ici.org/issues/fee/fm-v15n4.pdf (accessed December 20, 2006).

Investment Company Institute and Independent Directors Council. "Overview of Fund Governance Practices, 1994–2004," 2006. http://ici.org/pdf/rpt_fund_gov_practices.pdf (accessed December 20, 2006).

Investment Company Institute and Securities Industry Association. "Equity Ownership in America: 2005." http://www.sia.com/research/pdf/EquityOwnership05.pdf (accessed June 28, 2006).

Investment Management Association. *Review of the Governance Arrangements of United Kingdom Authorised Collective Investment Schemes*, February 2005. http://www.investmentuk.org/news/research/2005/topic/unit_trusts/cisgovernance.pdf (accessed December 22, 2006).

Kahn, Alfred E. *The Economics of Regulation: Principles and Institutions.* Vols. 1 and 2. Cambridge, MA: MIT Press, 1988.

Kertz, Consuelo L., and Paul J. Simko. "Mutual Fund Investing and Tax Uncertainty: The Need for New Disclosures." *Stanford Journal of Law, Business, and Finance* 7 (Autumn 2001): 103–130.

Khorana, Ajay, and Henri Servaes. "Conflicts of Interest and Competition in the Mutual Fund Industry," July 2004. http://ssrn.com/abstract=240596 (accessed December 20, 2006).

Lauricella, Tom. "Independent Directors Strike Back." *Wall Street Journal*, July 5, 2006.

Lauricella, Tom, Monica Langley, and Susan Pulliam. "Spitzer Gambit May Alter Fund-Fee Debate." *Wall Street Journal*, December 11, 2003.

Lemke, Thomas P., Gerald T. Lins, and A. Thomas Smith III. *Regulation of Investment Companies.* New York: Matthew Bender & Co., Inc., 1995.

Lipper. "A Comparison of Mutual Fund Expenses across the Atlantic." Lipper Fund*Industry* Insight Reports, September 2005.

———.*Global Themes in the Mutual Fund Industry—2005: A Review of the Global Pooled Investment Management Industry.* Lipper Research Study, February 2006.

———. *Taxes in the Mutual Fund Industry—2006: Assessing the Impact of Taxes on Shareholders' Returns.* Lipper Research Study, April 2006.

London, Paul A. *The Competition Solution: The Bipartisan Secret behind American Prosperity.* Washington, DC: AEI Press, 2005.

Lybecker, Martin E. "Enhanced Corporate Governance for Mutual Funds: A Flawed Concept That Deserves Serious Reconsideration." *Washington University Law Quarterly* 83 (2005): 1045–1092.

Malkiel, Burton G. 1996. *A Random Walk Down Wall Street*, 6th ed. New York: W. W. Norton & Company.

Markham, Jerry W. 2006. Mutual Funds and Other Collective Investment Mediums—A Comparative Analysis of Their Regulation and Governance, http://law.bepress.com/cgi/viewcontent.cgi?article=6341&context=expresso   (accessed March 6, 2007).

Money Management Institute. "Second Quarter Data, 2006." http://www.moneyinstitute.com/downloads/2006/09/2q06numbers.pdf (accessed January 12, 2007).

———. "SMA Assets Reach Record $805.8 Billion in 3Q 2006." http://www.moneyinstitute.com/downloads/2006/12/3q06pressrelease.pdf (accessed January 12, 2007).

Montgomery, John. Statement before the House Financial Services Committee Subcommittee on Capital Markets, Insurance, and Government Sponsored Enterprises.

Hearing, "Mutual Fund Industry Practices and Their Effect on Individual Investors," March 12, 2003. 108th Cong., 1st sess. (available through LexisNexis).

President's Working Group on Financial Markets. "Hedge Funds, Leverage, and the Lessons of Long-Term Capital Management," April 1999. http://www.ustreas.gov/press/releases/reports/hedgfund.pdf (accessed February 14, 2007)

Roye, Paul F. "Critical Issues for Investment Company Directors." Remarks before the Mutual Fund Directors Forum Fifth Annual Policy Conference, Washington, DC, February 17, 2005. http://www.sec.gov/news/speech/spch021705pfr.htm (accessed January 11, 2007).

Samuelson, Paul A., and William D. Nordhaus. *Economics*. 18th ed. New York: McGraw-Hill Irwin, 2005.

Saunders, Richard. Remarks, AEI conference, "The Regulation and Structure of Collective Investment Vehicles Outside the United States," Washington, DC, May 18, 2006. Transcript available at http://www.aei.org/event1318 (accessed February 26, 2007).

SEC v. Capital Gains Research Bureau, Inc. 375 U.S.180 (1963).

Shiller, Robert J. "The Life-Cycle Personal Accounts Proposal for Social Security: An Evaluation." Working Paper 11300, National Bureau of Economic Research, Cambridge, MA, April 2005. http://www.nber.org/papers/w11300 (accessed December 14, 2006).

Siegel, Jeremy J. *The Future for Investors: Why the Tried and the True Triumph Over the Bold and the New*. New York: Crown Business, 2005.

Slater, Robert. *John Bogle and the Vanguard Experiment: One Man's Quest to Transform the Mutual Fund Industry*. Chicago: Irwin Professional Publishing, 1996.

Swensen, David F. *Unconventional Success: A Fundamental Approach to Personal Investment*. New York: Free Press, 2005.

Tkac, Paula A. 2004. Mutual Funds: Temporary Problem or Permanent Morass? *Economic Review* 89 (Fourth Quarter): 1–21.

———. 2005. Remarks at the AEI conference, An Economist's View of Mutual Fund Regulation, April 14, Washington, DC. Transcript available at www.aei.org/event1284 (accessed March 2, 2007).

U.S. Congress. House. Joint Economic Committee. "Encouraging Personal Saving and Investment: Changing the Tax Treatment of Unrealized Capital Gains," June 2000. http://www.house.gov/jec/tax/mutual/mutual.pdf (accessed October 10, 2006).

———. Senate. Committee on Banking and Currency. *Investment Company Act of 1940 and Investment Advisers Act of 1940*. 76th Cong., 3rd sess., 1940. S. Rep. 1775.

———. *Investment Company Amendments Act of 1969*. 91st Cong., 1st sess., 1969. S. Rep. 184.

U.S. General Accounting Office. "Mutual Fund Fees: Additional Disclosure Could Encourage Price Competition," June 2000. http://www.gao.gov/archive/2000/gg00126.pdf (accessed December 18, 2006).

U.S. Securities and Exchange Commission. Investment Trusts and Investment Companies. Washington, DC: U.S. Government Printing Office, 1939–1940.

———. Public Policy Implications of Investment Company Growth. 89th Cong., 2nd sess., 1966. H. Rep. 2337.

———. "Investment Company Act Release 12888," December 10, 1982. Available through Westlaw (1982 WL 523380).

———. Consolidated Disclosure of Mutual Fund Expenses. Investment Company Act Release 16244 (February 1, 1988).{{AU:Federal Register data to add?}}

———. Role of Independent Directors of Investment Companies. Investment Company Act Release 24816 (January 2, 2001). Federal Register 66 (10): 3734–68.

———. Actively Managed Exchange-Traded Funds. Investment Company Act Release 25258 (November 8, 2001). http://www.sec.gov/rules/concept/ic-25258.htm (accessed January 9, 2007).

———. Confirmation Requirements and Point of Sale Disclosure Requirements for Transactions in Certain Mutual Funds and Other Securities, and Other Confirmation Requirement Amendments, and Amendments to the Registration Form for Mutual Funds. Investment Company Act Release 26341 (January 29, 2004). Federal Register 69 (27): 6438–98.

———. Shareholder Reports and Quarterly Portfolio Disclosure of Registered Management Investment Companies. Investment Company Act Release 26372 (February 27, 2004). Federal Register 69 (46): 11244–73.

———. Investment Company Governance. Investment Company Act Release 26520 (July 27, 2004). Federal Register 69 (147): 46378–93.

———. Point of Sale Disclosure Requirements and Confirmation Requirements for Transactions in Mutual Funds, College Savings Plans, and Certain Other Securities, and Amendments to the Registration Form for Mutual Funds. Investment Company Act Release 26778 (February 28, 2005). Federal Register 70 (42): 10521-57.

———. Prohibition of Fraud by Advisers to Certain Pooled Investment Vehicles; Accredited Investors in Certain Private Investment Vehicles. Investment Advisers Act Release 2576 (December 27, 2006). http://www.sec.gov/rules/proposed/2006/33-8766.pdf (accessed January 9, 2007).

U.S. Securities and Exchange Commission, Division of Investment Management. Protecting Investors: A Half-Century of Investment Company Regulation. Washington, DC: U.S. Government Printing Office, 1992.

———. Report on Mutual Fund Fees and Expenses, December 2000. www.sec.gov/news/studies/feestudy.htm (accessed December 20, 2006).

Wallison, Peter J. "Landmark Ruling." AEI Financial Services Outlook, May 2006. http://www.aei.org/publication24303 (accessed October 12, 2006).

———. "Groundhog Day: Reliving Deregulation Debates." AEI Financial Services Outlook, October 2006. http://www.aei.org/publication25034 (accessed January 18, 2007).

Weil, Roman L. "Allocations of Cost and Revenue." In Handbook of Cost Management, 2nd ed. Edited by Roman L. Weil and Michael W. Maher. Hoboken, NJ: John Wiley & Sons, 2005.

West, Stephen K. *The Investment Company Industry in the 1990's.* Report for the Investment Company Institute. Washington, DC: Investment Company Institute, March 1990.

Wharton School of Finance and Commerce. *A Study of Mutual Funds.* 87th Cong., 2nd sess., 1962. H. Rep. 2274.

White, Sam, and Todd Smurl. "Get Your Adviser to Open Up." *Forbes.com*, December 27, 2006. http://www.forbes.com/investoreducation/2006/12/27/open-architecture-smartleaf-pf-invedu-in_sw_1227soapbox_inl.html (accessed January 12, 2007).

Winston, Clifford W. "Economic Deregulation: Days of Reckoning for Microeconomists." *Journal of Economic Literature* 31 (September 1993): 1263

About the Authors

Peter J. Wallison is a senior fellow at the American Enterprise Institute, where he also co-directs AEI's Project on Financial Market Deregulation. He served as general counsel of the United States Treasury Department (1981–85), and subsequently as White House counsel to President Ronald Reagan (1986–87). Between 1972 and 1976, he served first as special assistant to New York Governor Nelson A. Rockefeller and, subsequently, as counsel to Mr. Rockefeller when he was vice president of the United States.

Mr. Wallison is the author of *Ronald Reagan: The Power of Conviction and the Success of His Presidency* (Westview Press, 2002). He is also the author of *Back From the Brink* (AEI Press, 1990), a proposal for a private deposit insurance system, and co-author of *Nationalizing Mortgage Risk: The Growth of Fannie Mae and Freddie Mac* (AEI Press, 2000) and *The GAAP Gap: Corporate Disclosure in the Internet Age* (AEI Press, 2000). He is also the editor of *Optional Federal Chartering and Regulation of Insurance Companies* (AEI Press, 2000), and *Serving Two Masters, Yet Out of Control: Fannie Mae and Freddie Mac* (AEI Press, 2001).

Robert E. Litan is vice president for research and policy at the Kauffman Foundation, a senior fellow in the Economic Studies and Global Studies Programs at the Brookings Institution, and co-director of the AEI-Brookings Joint Center on Regulatory Studies. Dr. Litan and Mr. Wallison previously co-authored *The GAAP Gap: Corporate Disclosure in the Internet Age* (AEI Press, 2000).

Dr. Litan is the author, co-author, or co-editor of more than 30 books and 200 articles on financial and economic topics. He formerly was vice president and director of economic studies at Brookings, an associate director of the Office of Management and Budget, deputy assistant attorney general in the Antitrust Division at the Department of Justice, a consultant for the Treasury Department, a member of the Commission on the Causes of the Savings and Loan Crisis, and a staff economist at the President's Council of Economic Advisers.

Index